Muslims Counter Trumpism

L. ALI KHAN

L. Ali Khan

DEDICATION

This book is dedicated to American Muslims, European Muslims, African Muslims, South Asian Muslims, Arab Muslims, Hispanic Muslims, those who are born Muslims, and those who accept Islam through free will.

L. Ali Khan

Contents

ACKNOWLEDGMENTS

Writing is a solitary mission. Muses, angels, fairies, and demons
bring ideas with cloudy texture and I shape them.

L. Ali Khan

INTRODUCTION

This book is a pool of essays written over a period of more than a year, starting from the days when Donald Trump began to emerge as a strong contestant in the 2016 presidential race. Trump's anti-Islamic rhetoric touched a nerve with the American voters; and, encouraged by polls, Trump proposed to ban the entry of *all* Muslims into the United States. From thereon, Trumpism turns into a form of Islamophobia.

Trumpism is much larger than Trump. Since June 2015 when Trump announced his candidacy for president, Trump had embraced the Neocon dogma of highlighting Islam and Muslims as the U.S. enemies. His stance against the Syrian refugees as potential terrorists reinforced the American fears prompted by the Neocons that Muslims will physically destroy the United States. The sporadic terrorist attacks perpetrated by Muslims in America were exaggerated beyond proportionality to validate the critiques of Islam as an anti-Western, imperialistic faith.

The Neocons under President George W. Bush, many of whom wrote anti-Islamic books and opinion pieces for the *New York Times* and the *Washington Post*, were determined to paint Islam as an intrinsically violent religion. They argued that Muslim militants are addicted to violence and that they will commit acts of terrorism even if they run out of geopolitical grievances, such as the occupation of Palestine, Iraq, Kashmir, and Afghanistan. Whereas the Neocons were mostly Jewish, the Trumpists are mostly Christians.

Trumpism developed the art of vilification. Just as the white settlers stigmatized Native Americans as savages, the Trumpists, including Trump and his men and women, brand Muslims as terrorists. The very word terrorist has turned synonymous with Muslim militant. The Neocons promoted wars against Muslim countries, particularly in the Middle East. Unfortunately, many autocratic Arab rulers, fearful of their own fragile regimes, sided with the Neocons in branding Muslim militants as vicious terrorists, thus discounting the rationale of liberation movements in occupied Muslim lands. The Arab rulers who supported the struggle for liberation and the right of self-defense were overthrown and murdered.

The war on terrorism has caused a fundamental shift in the right to self-defense. The occupiers and invaders have been successful in changing the international law of self-defense, an inalienable right enshrined in the United Nations Charter. The right of self-defense of an occupied people, such as the Palestinians, has been taken away and gifted to the occupiers. Consequently, Israel is granted the right to self-defense that it may enforce through bombings, assassinations, and demolitions of family houses of defiant militants. However, any armed struggle to liberate the land from occupiers is now regarded as terrorism.

This shift in the concept of self-defense (now belonging to the occupiers and invaders) benefits nations that wish to suppress the liberation movements of self-determination. India is gratified to see the liberation movement in Kashmir called terrorism. Likewise, the U.S. fully supports the new concept of self-defense as it invades country after country in the Middle East and elsewhere. Even political dictatorships promptly use the label of terrorism to condemn any opposition that demands a representative form of government.

Trumpism, much like its predecessor Neoconism, plays into the self-interest of the U.S. warfare establishment that sees war as an attractive evil. The Pentagon, the CIA, and the weapons industry constitute the core of the warfare establishment. Billions of dollars are invested in the invention and manufacturing of weapons from bombs to aircrafts to missiles to cyber-warfare systems. The warfare industry needs to sell weapons.

The warfare establishment sponsors wars just as drug dealers sponsor addictions. The warfare industry has tremendous influence over the U.S. foreign policy, and the perpetuation of warfare is conducive to a thriving weapons industry. Accordingly, the warfare establishment germinates and aggravates regional conflicts involving nations that can afford to buy expensive warfare systems. Saudi Arabia, Japan, South Korea, and India are drawn into regional armed conflicts and Trumpism prompts them to buy "defensive weapons."

In addition to bracing international warfare, Trumpism fosters hateful racism, an enduring social pathology in the United States.

Despite good faith efforts in many domains, including law, racism refuses to go away from the American mindset. Racism continues to find new target communities. In addition to Native Americans, Africans, the Italians, the Irish, and the Japanese, numerous other communities face racism perpetrated by a fractional population of the Anglo vintage.

Ironically, the prior victims of racism join the perpetrators of racism. For example, the Irish Catholics, once the target of Anglo racism, are leading the racist agenda against the Hispanics and other vulnerable communities. Likewise, many American Jews influential in the media and academy foment Islamophobia, ignoring the fact that hatred against any religious group can easily be turned around against the Jews. It is in this context that racist attacks against the Jews have escalated under Trumpism, even though Trump and his cohorts come across as strong supporters of Israel and American Jews.

Muslims countering Trumpism both inside and outside the United States summon classical Islamic consciousness that refuses to accept victimhood. It has been customary in America that the persecuted communities adopt victimhood. For example, the African American communities, the most persecuted people over the centuries, have been forced to view their lives through the dark prisms of racism. Even the best and the brightest African Americans lament being the victims of racism. President Obama too bemoaned that racism was the single most agony he suffered in occupying the office of the president.

Relying on victimhood is not the Islamic way. Islam has contributed one thing unique to human civilization --an indomitable will to be free and fearless under adverse circumstances. Islam teaches its followers two important lessons: One, be patient under hardship; two, do something to fight adversity. Thus, Islamic consciousness teaches patient determinism to overcome the difficulty. This mindset does not accept slavery, surrender, persecution, occupation, discrimination, or any form of inferiority. It is this Islamic mindset that attracts subjugated women, prisoners, low castes, social outcasts, and other marginalized communities to accept Islam.

Accordingly, American Muslims do not accept second-class citizenship. They work hard to educate their children to become engineers, doctors, accountants, journalists, lawyers, and other middle-class professionals. They are loyal to the United States, as other Muslims are loyal to their own countries. They fight for the United States as other Muslims fight for their own countries. But American Muslims do not just complain that they are not treated equally. They sue the bastards. They refuse to be harassed at the airports. They criticize unjust laws. They stand with the downtrodden. They decline to join the oppressors or the perpetrators of racism. Muslims are anti-fragile, a concept under which an entity thrives under adversity.

This anti-fragile mindset is also operative at the international level. For example, Pakistan, a country that remains in perpetual turmoil, has shown to be anti-fragile. Despite huge security problems emanating from the invasion of Afghanistan, Pakistan has gradually emerged on the world scene as a fine nation with tremendous intellectual and creative potential. Likewise, Iran facing life-threatening economic sanctions have shown to be antifragile, not just resilient. Trumpism cannot break or bend the Islamic anti-fragile mentality.

This book is written as the first draft of Trumpism from a Muslim perspective. The chapters are commentaries in response to events related to Trumpism. The thematic correlation among various chapters is somewhat inaudible. The topics covered are multidimensional, and commentaries are more than journalistic reporting of events. The analysis moves from hardnosed logic to light-hearted humor, such as the chapter on whether Trump is a Muslim. In sum, the book is written as a piece of raw history that later generations may consult in articulating a more credible view of Trumpism as related to Islam and Muslims.

The book ends with a rather pessimistic note: "At this time of weakness both home and abroad, the slogan of *Make America Great Again* sounds much like the Siren Song in Homer's Odyssey. It is tragic entrapment for a shipwreck. Students of history know how nations squander to lose their God-gifted competitive military, economic, and moral advantage. The fall of the United States, and its possible dismemberment, will be yet another heart-rending story in human history."

1 Muslim Ban

Friday, January 27, 2017, is the day when the United States President Donald Trump took the first step toward the official persecution of Muslims in the United States and around the world. This day, Trump signed an executive order banning the nationals of seven Muslim countries, five in the Middle East (Iran, Iraq, Libya, Syria, and Yemen) and two in Africa (Sudan, Somalia). The executive order was not limited to the admission of refugees. Even legal immigrants (green card holders and persons with other visas) from these countries returning to the United States were refused entry, causing immense emotional distress to the blocked individuals and their families waiting at U.S. airports. On Saturday, a federal judge blocked the implementation of the executive order with respect to the people stranded at the U.S. airports. However, The Department of Homeland Security has vowed to enforce the executive order.

Within hours of the signing of the executive order, a mosque in Texas was torched and completely destroyed. Hateful crimes against Muslims in America have been on the rise ever since Donald Trump and other Republican leaders (Ted Cruz and Mario Rubio) have freely employed incendiary rhetoric against the so-called radical Islamic terrorism, a phrase that implicates the religion of Islam as a primary contributing factor in the commission of terrorism.

According to the Pew Research, the crimes against Muslims have been on the rise in the past thirty-six months, and anti-Muslim crimes include property damage as well as intimidation crimes such as threats of bodily harm. The scene of Muslim women -- after their hijabs are forcibly ripped apart in public or their husbands detained at the airports or their families arbitrarily disembarked from domestic flights -- is emerging as the poster-scene of persecution.

Symptoms are sprouting that President Trump is plotting to follow the example of President Andrew Jackson (1829-37). Chief White House strategist Steve Bannon called Trump's inauguration speech "Jacksonian." President Trump hung a portrait of Andrew Jackson in the Oval Office, invoking deliberate connections with the "populist'" and "patriotic" policies and mindset of his distant predecessor.

In addition to slavery, one of the saddest chapters in American history is the removal of Native Americans from their ancestral lands. President Jackson who coined the predatory aphorism that "to the victors belong the spoils" was the most forceful president in seizing the lands from the Native Americans and granting them to the White settlers. Jackson defied even the Supreme Court decision to relocate the reluctant tribes, causing the death of nearly sixteen thousand Cherokees under the atrocious conditions of the "Trail of Tears."

What President Jackson did to Native Americans, President Trump is proposing to do to Mexicans and Muslims. Removal is the key concept that ties Trump with Jackson. Mexicans must be removed from the United States and Muslims must not be allowed entry into the United States. The theme is the same: Native Americans were savages, Mexicans are criminals, and Muslims are terrorists. A peaceful and prosperous America will be "beautiful" and thrive once unwanted groups are removed, killed, or subjugated.

It is a well-established historical fact that the persecution begins with the rhetoric of dehumanization. President George Washington said: "Indians and wolves are both beasts of prey, tho' they differ in shape." Thomas Jefferson, the author of the Declaration of Independence, remarked: "If ever we are constrained to lift the hatchet against any tribe, we will never lay it down till that tribe is exterminated, or driven beyond the Mississippi... in war, they will kill some of us; we shall destroy them all." Andrew Jackson talked much like a race-supremacist: "They (Native Americans) have neither the intelligence, the industry, the moral habits, nor the desire of improvement which are essential to any favorable change in their condition." This rhetoric paved the way for the dehumanization and dispossession of Native Americans.

The rhetoric of the Trump team against Islam, not just Muslims, has departed from the constraints that previous presidents have observed while condemning terrorism. The Trump team's rhetoric is overreaching refusing to draw distinctions between ordinary Muslims and Muslim militants. "Islam hates us," was the broad generalization that Trump used to endorse "We have to the play the game at a much tougher level than we're playing it." National Security Adviser Michael Flynn was blunt and hateful: "Islamism a **vicious cancer** inside the body of 1.7 billion people on this planet and it has to be excised." Jeff Sessions, the incoming federal attorney general, calls Islam a "toxic ideology" and has little problem with registering Muslims in the United States.

The people of the United States are divided over the maltreatment of Muslims. Trump supporters do not view favorably Islam or Muslims in the United States. They may not support but will remain silent if persecution escalates. However, millions of Americans, white, black, men, women, will oppose any oppression of Muslims as a community. The protests challenging Trump's executive order at various U.S. airports and the supportive speeches by the mayors of New York and Boston indicate that times are gone when an entire community could be dehumanized and tormented. The U.S. courts, including conservative judges, are unlikely to allow a complete destruction of the Bill of Rights, declaring Islam as a religion non-grata. The additional factor that over a billion Muslims across the world are watching Trump and his men cannot be ignored in the calculus of persecution.

2 Shariah Deportations

Newt Gingrich, who holds a Ph.D. in European History and is thus a presumptively educated man, has delivered yet another questionable statement: "We should frankly test every person here who is of a Muslim background and if they believe in Sharia, they should be deported." Over the decades, Gingrich is known for making unintelligent speeches, without weighing the consequences of his thoughtless philosophies.

In 2011, Gingrich said: "I am convinced that if we do not decisively win the struggle over the nature of America, by the time they're my age, they will be in a secular atheist country, potentially one dominated by radical Islamists." Gingrich has not yet explained how an atheist transformation of America will be dominated by radical Islamists for whom a belief in One God is central to faith. Driven by an inflated self-concept of competence, Gingrich says things and then spends a lifetime retracting his foolery.

Gingrich's proposal of making belief as a ground for deportation cannot be taken seriously. Of course, illegal Muslim immigrants can be deported without any reason. But deporting legal immigrants on grounds of belief will be a radical development in immigration law. The immensity of the Gingrich proposal ignores that millions of American Muslims are citizens of the United States, both naturalized and native-born. Under the proposal, American Muslims born in the United States, like Representative Keith Ellison, who might believe in the Shariah, will stand deportation. But deported to where remains an unresolved riddle. In making dubious statements, Former Speaker of the House Gingrich comes across as a graceless leader who, as a prior lawmaker, should know better.

It appears that Gingrich, like some other scared critics of Islam, has a poor understanding of the Shariah. The critics of Islam identify Shariah with terrorism, burqa, and harsh criminal punishments such as stoning for adultery. The fear of the Shariah is widespread, particularly among white male circles, as is the fear of African Americans. Prompted by panic, prejudice, and phobia, some state legislators have passed constitutional amendments or legislation against the enforcement of Shariah in state courts, ignoring the First Amendment protections of religious freedom. Fortunately, the federal courts have struck down the attempts to de-legalize Shariah.

For practicing Muslims, Shariah is a set of beliefs and a code of rules that govern the daily life of individuals and families. Foremost, Shariah means a belief in One God and respect for prophets, including Abraham, Moses, and Jesus. Shariah regulates, among numerous things, the times of prayers, the rituals of prayers, the times of fasting in the month of Ramadhan, and the amount of mandatory charity annually dispensed to the poor and the needy.

Shariah also instructs Muslims to speak truthfully but gently, be kind to children, keep the aging and sick parents at home, respect the privacy of neighbors, refrain from cruelty to animals, reject adultery and take care of an ill spouse. The Shariah also carries the complicated rules of inheritance, trusts, donations, partnership, financing, arbitration, evidence, judicial ethics, and rational proof-based judgments. In the Middle centuries, the common law of England freely borrowed from the rules of the Shariah. Many Shariah rules are like Jewish law freely practiced and officially recognized in the United States.

The U.S. Constitution protects the free exercise of Islam, that is, protects the Shariah that Muslim families practice in living spiritually satisfying lives. For the most part, the Shariah and the Constitution are compatible. In matters of incompatibility, there is no possibility that the Shariah would modify the U.S. Constitution; or, the state and federal courts would enforce any elements of the Shariah that violate the Bill of Rights or any other deeply embedded legal values. Whipping up the fear that the Shariah undermines the U.S. Constitution is based on faulty assumptions and lack of knowledge.

If there is any danger to the integrity of the Constitution and American values of religious liberty, it comes from provocateurs like Trump, Cruz, and Gingrich. Many well-informed Americans, including Mike Pence, Trump's pick for the vice president, oppose the hatred against Islam and American Muslims trumped up by politicians, evangelists, neocons and other dubious characters.

3 Suing the Bastards

"Sue the bastards" is a catchy phrase invented in 1970 by Victor Yannacone, a U.S. lawyer and environmentalist, a trailblazer in cutting-edge litigation. The phrase, despite its critics, captures a sentiment for law-based empowerment against the hefty and mighty. Without fright, alarm, or vacillation, American Muslims are quietly 'suing the bastards" and asserting their civil liberties in courts - a quintessentially American thing to do. A review of cases decided in 2015 reveal how American Muslims are claiming, sometimes pro se and sometimes with the help of pro bono and fee-paid lawyers, their rights against discrimination, hostility, and harassment.

A symptomatic discrimination case, reported in Khan v. Hilton Worldwide, occurs at the Waldorf Astoria New York, a plush hotel located half a mile away from showy Trump Tower. In 2005, Ehsan Khan (no relation to the author) starts working as a "Café Attendant" at the Starbucks inside the Waldorf Astoria, owned by Hilton. For over five years, Khan works at the hotel to satisfaction of the management. In 2010, Khan hears a troubling interchange. A coworker says to the supervisor, "Why don't you like me? Is it because I'm Muslim?" The supervisor exclaims back, "Yes, it's because you are Muslim!" A disgusted Khan reports the incident to Hilton Human Resources. A few months later, Hilton retaliates and terminates Khan citing two bogus reasons. One, Khan has not paid for a coffee drink; two, Khan has remained on-site for an hour after signing out. Khan brings an employment retaliation lawsuit.

Just in 2015, hundreds of Muslim cases are working through state and federal courts. Here is a small sampling. A hijab-wearing American Muslim sues Abercrombie and Fitch Stores for discriminatory hiring practices and wins the case in the United States Supreme Court. A "dark-skinned" Iraqi Muslim sues Michigan Bell because the Bell manager has created a hostile work environment by calling the plaintiff a Taliban and "joking" that the plaintiff is learning to fly airplanes on an office graffiti depicting the Twin Towers. An American Muslim family from New Jersey sues JetBlue Airways when the family is removed from a flight after boarding the plane because their daughter, then 18 months old, is found to be on a no-fly list. Later, TSA issues a statement saying it has not flagged (the child) as being on the no-fly list.

American Muslims are aware of American history replete with traumatization of many communities. Native Americans, Africans, Hispanics, Mormons, Catholics, Greeks, Italians, Irish, and others, one after the other, have been disparaged as communities. "Help Wanted - Blank need not apply" has been the meta-slogan periodically filled with bigotry against ethnic and religious communities. Following the example of earlier battered communities, American Muslims are firm; they are not about to renounce their faith, rights, or way of life for fear of surveillance, entrapment, discrimination, hatred, violence, or social micro-aggressions they might encounter in the years to come. They stand rooted like palm trees in squalls of vicious winds.

American history liberates American Muslims to fight persecution through the apparatus of law. Us versus them, a devious theory, prevalent in predatory circles, undermines the wholesome development of laws and the constitution. American Muslims of all races, hues, national origins, and denominations feel in their hearts and minds that they are no different, neither superior nor inferior, from other nationals of the United States. Donald Trump, Mike Huckabee, Ted Cruz, Hillary Clinton, Carly Fiorina, or others —none of them— separately or jointly, own the United States any more than American Muslims. Anglicans, Baptists, Methodists, Seventh-day Adventists, Catholics, Mormons, Jews, or the followers of any other religion or atheism - none of them— separately or jointly, have constitutional rights and privileges, as do American Muslims.

Asserting constitutional rights in public spaces, female American Muslims walk freely, though cautiously, wearing modest clothes and hijab, just as other female Americans walk freely, though cautiously, wearing garments of their choice and faith obligations. Male American Muslims shave faces or don beards - stubble, full, ducktail, goatee, or extended goatee—as do other male Americans. Muslim children, boys and girls, go to schools, public and private, proud of their families and communities, much like other American children proud of their families and communities. Just as religious Americans recite holy Gospels, Torah, Book of Mormons, and other divine books, religious American Muslims recite the Qur'an, holy and noble.

American Muslims, including lawyers, physicians, engineers, cab drivers, and businessmen and businesswomen, realize that constitutional rights are not ornamental pieces for décor in privileged mansions. These rights make life possible and the potentials of life reachable. Physical security, right to spirituality, equal opportunity, freedom from government harassment including surveillance, these and other rights are the provisions of satisfying life. These rights mean a lot to all individuals and communities, powerful and powerless. These rights mean even more to battered communities, battered by hostility, stereotyping, insults, and intentional affliction of emotional distress.

Accessing courts is an act of courage. It is showing the mirror to the government, including its law enforcement agencies. When enforcement agencies and non-governmental bullies such as Muslim-bashing Donald Trump and Qur'an-burning Terry Jones or hate-spewing Fox News assault the peace and dignity of American Muslims, the constitutional rights of all American citizens are weakened. The courts may not always safeguard the rights of American Muslims. The history's indictment of U.S. courts demonstrates that even judges are not immune from prejudice and group-think. Yet, seeking remedies through courts and "suing the bastards" is therapeutic.

.

4 A Muslim in Trump Cabinet

It will be a stroke of genius for President-Elect Donald Trump to pick an American Muslim for his cabinet. This move will be a great gesture for connecting with 56 Muslim countries of the Organization of Islamic Cooperation, over 1.5 billion Muslims of the world, and recruiting American Muslims as allies against any possible threat to our national security. This move will also offset the anti-Islamic negativity associated with Michael Flynn and Steve Bannon.

An American Muslim picked for a cabinet portfolio must be a true believer in Islam, who performs daily prayers, fasts in the month of Ramadhan, gives charity and is kind-hearted and educated. An American Muslim just in name or one espousing questionable notions such as "moderate Islam" or "American Islam" will be utterly useless if not harmful to serving in the Trump cabinet. Vilifying Islam will not work and prolonging war with Muslims will bear no fruit. In the words of Chinese military general Sun Tzu, "There is no instance of a country having benefited from prolonged warfare." *See* The Art of War (5 BCE).

There are hundreds of thousands American Muslims, native-born and immigrant, with diverse racial and ethnic backgrounds and expertise –- men, women, Arabs, South Asians, African-Americans, Caucasians – who can promote American interests and American values in the Muslim world. An American Muslim, who is immigrant-citizen, will add even more credibility and complexity to the cabinet position -- much like Jewish-American Henry Kissinger or Polish-American Zbigniew Brzezinski, each serving as Secretary of State.

It is not uncommon for democracies to reach out to minorities and recruit them for cabinet positions to better manage domestic and international affairs. In 2001, Republican President George W. Bush chose Colin Powell and Condoleezza Rice, both African-Americans, as Secretary of State and National Security Advisor. In 2015, Canadian Prime Minister Justin Trudeau has picked four Indian-Canadians in the cabinet. He also picked Maryam Monsef, an Afghan-Canadian, and a Muslim born in an Iranian refugee camp, as Minister of Democratic Institutions.

So far, no American Muslim has served as a member of the United States President's cabinet. Goodwill, sagacity, and demands of international peace and security mandate that the United States connect with the vast Muslim world so that good sentiments prevail, misunderstandings are removed, and a new path is lit for the benefit of the world at large. Targeting Muslim communities abroad or American Muslims at home will achieve nothing but escalate violence, breed needless animosity, and further bruise the world with a thousand cuts.

Islamophobia will not solve the security problems of the United States. However, picking an American Muslim as a member of the cabinet will revolutionize the American mindset, sending a powerful message to all that Islam is a blessing for America and America is a beautiful home for Muslims as it has been for Christians, Jews, Hindus, and many other faith communities.

5 Trump's Holy War

In his inaugural address, President Trump singled out radical Islamic terrorism as the sole enemy. He did not even mention Russia or China as threats to the security or prosperity of the United States. In terse and clear words, Trump said: "We will reinforce old alliances and form new ones and unite the civilized world against radical Islamic terrorism, which we will eradicate from the face of the Earth." In fighting against radical Islamic terrorism, Trump asserted that "We will be protected by the great men and women of our military and law enforcement. And most importantly, we will be protected by God."

There are three points worth consideration to understand Trump's speech on radical Islamic terrorism. Each point is rooted in history and academic literature, and each point carries serious implications for the peace and security of the United States and the world.

First, radical Islamic terrorism is presented as a threat to "the civilized world." Historically, the phrase "civilized world" was coined in the era of colonialism to refer primarily to the European nations and by implication to the "uncivilized world" referred to Native Americans in Americas, slaves from Africa, and the colonized populations in Asia. Under contemporary standards of global discourse, the phrase "civilized world" is rarely used by diplomats, heads of states, or academic scholars. There is a new understanding that the world is blessed with numerous diverse civilizations, including the Islamic civilization that spans over centuries in all continents of the world. It is unclear whether President Trump includes fifty-six (56) Muslim countries as part of the civilized world.

Second, the phrase "radical Islamic terrorism" was invented to argue that Islamic violence emanates from the religion itself and not from any concrete geopolitical grievances for which Muslim militants are fighting in various parts of the world. The phrase "radical Islamic terrorism "was popular with neoconservatives who wanted to shift the focus from grievances to Islamic psychology. For example, the phrase implies that the Palestinians as Muslims are addicted to violence that has nothing to do with occupation or misery they face as a people. Likewise, the phrase would suggest that the Taliban as Muslims are hooked to religiously-inspired warfare and their violence has little to do with the invasion of Afghanistan. By adopting the phrase during his campaign and mention it in his inaugural speech, President Trump has bought into the idea that a radical version of Islam is inherently brutal and will find excuses to perpetrate violence throughout the world even after all the problems have been solved.

Third, Trump has added a holy war component to the eradication of radical Islamic terrorism from the face of the Earth. In addition to seeking protection from "the great men and women of our military," Trump claims that "we will be protected by God." This simply means that God is on the side of the United States in its wars against various nations and populations, particularly radical Islamic terrorism. This understanding of God's partisanship in human wars is the cardinal principle of the holy war whether the concept is invoked by Catholics, Protestants, Shias, Sunnis, or Shiv Sena.

A serious study of Islamic terrorism suggests that Muslim militancy originates in concrete geopolitical causes, including occupations and invasions. Muslim militants desert their families and children, forfeit their lives, and invite the wrath of mighty states because they are fighting the occupation of their lands, resources, or way of life. Unless the grievances factor is honestly included in the counter-terrorism equation, radical Islamic terrorism will not abate.

The phrase radical Islamic terrorism is overly provocative. It is a bad piece of rhetoric that does more harm than good. It implicates the religion of Islam, spawning hatred against ordinary Muslim families living in Western countries. The phrase also discourages peace-loving Muslims all over the world to join the fight against terrorism as they feel their religion is being maligned. As far as Muslim militants are concerned, they do not care whether they are called terrorists, radical Islamists, brutes, uncivilized, or any such phrases.

There are good reasons for all, including Americans, to criticize when Muslim militants openly and deliberately violate the laws of war. Destroying ancient temples, Sufi shrines, ramming trucks into civilian crowds, bombing cities, and threatening nuclear holocaust, all these and other acts are condemnable. Muslims are obligated to openly and unreservedly condemn when Muslim militants commit such atrocities that have nothing to do with any version of Islam.

Finally, bringing God into the fight is ill-advised. For centuries, God is presented as a sponsor of violence and warfare. Trump has ruled out the possibility that God is indifferent to human wars and that God does not condone or take part in cluster bombings, drone attacks, or the use of nuclear weapons against any cities.

6 Sufi Shrines

The trial of a Muslim militant for destroying historical monuments in Timbuktu (Mali) is under way before the International Criminal Court (ICC) in The Hague. Ahmed Al-Faqi Al-Mehdi, known as Abou Tourab, is not contesting the charges of taking part in the destruction of shrines built for Muslim Sufis in the legendary city of Timbuktu, a center of world civilization from the 13th to the 16th centuries, long before, for example, the United States (1776) came into being and long before the Eiffel Tower (1889) and Taj Mahal (1643) were built. Abou Tourab is charged with war crimes under the Rome Statute, a global treaty that establishes the ICC to prosecute generals, presidents, prime ministers, kings, and queens for commanding the commission of genocide, war crimes, crimes against humanity, and the crime of aggression.

The international criminal court is a promising institution for enforcing high-level accountability even though so far, regrettably, it has reached only African leaders and Muslim militants. Despite this lopsidedness, however, it will be a mistake to argue that the

Rome Statute is the Western law imposed on Africa or the Muslim world. Many African and Muslim states are willing parties to the Rome Statute while some Western states, including the United States, are not.

This commentary explains that the Rome Statute is compatible with the Shariah – the Islamic law derived from the Qur'an and the Prophet's Sunnah. The Shariah allows the prosecution, conviction, and punishment of Muslims, whether they are militants or state officials, who destroy historical monuments belonging to any people, religion, era, or civilization.

It is no historical fluke that for hundreds of years, the ancient pre-Islamic monuments located in Egypt, Syria, Iraq, Jordan, Pakistan, and elsewhere in Muslim lands have been protected by Muslim rulers and Muslim communities. Here and there, some misguided Muslims have breached the Shariah and destroyed non-Islamic monuments and houses of worship.

The ICC is prosecuting Abou Tourab for destroying Muslim monuments in Mali, a Muslim state. However, the Shariah would allow the prosecution and punishment of Muslims destroying even non-Muslim monuments. For example, the Shariah would indict the Taliban who demolished the Buddha statues in Afghanistan as it would indict Islamic State Caliph Al-Baghdadi under whose command the temple of Baal, a pre-Islamic deity, has been wrecked in Syria.

Undoubtedly, Islam offers a unique concept of One God who bears no resemblance to any ethereal or material creatures including human beings. The non-anthropomorphic pure monotheism of Islam intensifies prohibition against worshipping saints, Swamis, and Sufis, or reducing God to any representative material manifestation such as idols and images. This concept of One God – a remarkable contribution to the annals of monotheism – cannot be forced upon non-Muslims for the Qur'an prohibits compelling non-Muslims to subscribe to the Islamic belief system (2:256).

Absolute tolerance of all religious communities, including polytheists and atheists, is an inseverable part of Islamic faith binding on all Muslims. Any deviation from this obligation is a crime under the Shariah. If a group of militants believes that certain faith communities within Islam, such as shrine-visitors, are non-Muslims, the militants remain under the Shariah obligation not to harm the shrines. Similarly, the temples of Baha'is, the mosques of Qadianis, and the imambaras of Shias, all are inviolable and worthy of respect. No sect of Islam has been empowered to pass judgments on other sects.

Destroying temples, synagogues, and churches of non-Muslim communities is also strictly prohibited for they too are sacred houses where God is worshiped. Note that the Qur'an uses the word masjid in a generic sense even though in popular usage the word masjid is used for Muslim houses of worship. Under the Qur'an's divine etymology, any house of worship of a Muslim or non-Muslim faith community is a masjid. "O children of Adam, clothe yourself decently when you attend *kulli masjidin* (houses of worship) (7:31)." The intended audience of this verse is the entire humanity and not just Muslims.

Furthermore, what is not permitted in peacetimes is also not permitted in war times. The Islamic law of war allows fighting for just causes because Islam is a peaceful but not a pacifist religion.

However, the Shariah places obligations on Muslim warriors to observe a strict humanitarian code of warfare founded on proportionality, compassion, forgiveness, and minimal damage to property. This code prohibits any wanton destruction of villages, water supplies, crops, and houses of worship. The Islamic State (ISIL) is loathed by Muslims across the world because of its brutality, torture, demolitions, and utter disregard of the Shariah humanitarian law.

The Shariah places obligations on Muslim warriors to observe a strict humanitarian code of warfare founded on proportionality, compassion, forgiveness, and minimal damage to property.

The prosecution of Al-Mehdi is not only appropriate but required under the Shariah. Al-Mehdi's confession of guilt is consistent with the Shariah. Since the Rome Statute is for the most part compatible with the Shariah, Muslim rulers must fully cooperate in the prosecution of misguided militants who harm the common heritage of humankind.

It is also hoped that the ICC would broaden its prosecutorial net to indict the leaders of powerful Western states, who unleash military actions in Muslim states without any regard for the destruction of historical monuments located in these states. Western leaders who start illegal wars and endanger the destruction of world heritage monuments must be brought to justice under the Rome Statute.

7 Harassment at Airports

Ever since President Trump signed an executive order banning individuals from seven Muslim-majority countries, reports of harassment at US entry points, including airports and road crossings, have inundated newspapers, news websites, and social media. Tourists, legal immigrants, even US naturalized and US-born citizens have reported degrading treatment, humiliation, and intimidation by US Customs and Border Protection (CBP) officials. In addition to travelers with Muslim names from all over the world including European Muslims, non-Muslim visitors have also been detained and subjected to pointless questioning.

For example, French Holocaust scholar Henry Rousso was detained for more than 10 hours at the Houston airport. Mem Fox, an eminent Australian writer of children's books, was detained at the Los Angeles airport. "I have never in my life been spoken to with such insolence, treated with such disdain, with so many insults, and with so much gratuitous impoliteness," Fox said. Of course, the degradation of Muslims arriving at US airports has been widespread. The son of legendary boxer <u>Muhammad Ali</u> was detained for hours at Fort Lauderdale airport after he was returning from speaking at a Black History Month event in Jamaica. He, a US-born citizen, was asked whether he was a Muslim.

Harassment is a well-known legal concept in the US. Harassment is both criminal and civil. As a general concept, criminal harassment means a course of conduct, including words and gestures, knowingly directed at an individual to alarm, annoy, torment, or terrorize the targeted person. Civil harassment is a form of discrimination, practiced in employment and housing, based on race, religion, sexual preference, national origin, or gender. Federal laws prohibit civil harassment where state laws prohibit both civil and criminal harassment.

There is no federal law specifically prohibiting CBP officials from "harassment" of travelers arriving at the US points of entry. In fact, the CBP officials at points of entry have more powers than police officers on the streets. Unlike police officers, the CBP officials need not have a probable cause to ask intruding questions to incoming travelers, nor a reasonable suspicion to search their luggage. They may do so at will for their primary responsibility is to prevent the entry of persons and goods that pose threat to national security or violate the US immigration, agricultural, monetary, or other laws.

The reported cases of harassment by the CBP officials are inconsistent with the "national goal" that in 2015 the Departments of Homeland Security and Commerce proposed to President Obama: "The United States will provide a best-in-class arrival experience, as compared to our global competitors, to an ever-increasing number of international visitors while maintaining the highest standards of national security."

There could be several reasons why the CBP is engaging in a course of conduct incompatible with providing a best-in-class arrival experience as promised in the 2015 proposal:

President Trump or Secretary John Kelly of Homeland Security may have abandoned the 2015 goal, (even though the policy is still displayed at the CBP website), now focusing more on national security and less on the commercial benefits that flow from international visitors. The stories of CBP harassment might reduce the already dwindling number of international travelers to the US.

The reported stories of intense questioning by the CBP officials are getting more than usual press coverage because of the illegal executive order banning refugees and other travelers.

The CBP officials conducting secondary inspections (detention, detailed questioning, and luggage searches) are not well-trained in the effective but dignified questioning of international visitors including US legal immigrants and citizens coming back home.

Whatever is causing the perceived and actual harassment at the US points of entry, concrete consequences flow from the negative perception among the peoples of the world that the US has turned into a land of disrespect, discrimination, and deportations.

First, fewer visitors from Muslim and non-Muslim countries will undertake expensive trips to the US. They are unlikely to spend money to be degraded at US airports. Visitors wishing to have a good time without being abused and harassed in the host country. Once a country loses goodwill, most international travelers think twice before visiting there.

Second, fewer new students will opt to study in US colleges and universities. Already, China is attracting hundreds of thousands of foreign students. Likewise, specialty occupations might also fail to recruit skilled professionals. As the 2015 report rightfully points out there are global competitors who wish to divert traffic from the US to their own countries.

The Department of Homeland Security and CBP need to understand that they are doing a disfavor to the economy and reputation of the US by their over-zealous detention and questioning of international visitors. They should presume, unless there are apparent contra-indications, that international travelers with valid visas obtained from US consulates and embassies located in foreign countries are innocent travelers and not a potential security threat. This presumption applies even more strongly to legal immigrants and US-born and naturalized citizens returning home after vacation or business travel.

The President's new executive order on March 6, though it excludes Iraq from its coverage, is still focused on Muslim countries. Like the previous executive order, it too is likely to make Muslims traveling to the United States from all countries more vulnerable to CBP vetting procedures. The harassment stories at US points of entry will multiply again.

8 Trump Walls

Much like some other animals, humans are wired to build separation markers, known as fences, borders, and walls. Leg-lifting dogs urinate to mark their territory. Rabbits claim their ground by depositing fecal pellets. Rodents rely on the quantitative model of urination (more pee) to "countermark" an area claimed by rival rodents. Animals mark territory mostly for defending their food and mates. Human walls carry a complex mixture of territorial, psychological, pathological, and predatory motives. The objective to build walls varies from self-enclosure to adverse possession of someone else's territory. Furthermore, populations build walls to mark and countermark their national, religious, ethnic, and racial identities.

Since time immemorial, the Chinese had been building walls at the northern border against the Mongols. Seven hundred years ago, the Ming dynasty unified and fortified the ancient walls into the first momentous territorial wall (over thirteen thousand miles long) known to human history –the Great Wall of China. Like the

Chinese, the Trojans built walls to protect the city of Troy. The Romans built a lengthy wall (73 miles) to safeguard the colonized Britannia from Scottish invasions. The ruins of ancient walls have survived in Iraq, Zimbabwe, and Peru.

The 21st century is witnessing a recharged revival in building walls in the name of national security. The adage, poeticized and ridiculed by Robert Frost, declares that "good fences make good neighbors." Yet, the new walls face resistance, even condemnation, from critics. In 2004, the International Court of Justice condemned the Israeli wall built in the West Bank, calling it a predatory land grab. In 2016, President Trump, a realtor by vocation, promised to build a 30-foot-high "beautiful wall" along the border with Mexico. Vincent Fox, the former President of Mexico, denounced the proposal as a "fucken wall." India is planning to build security walls on the borders with Pakistan and Bangladesh. Pakistan is building a wall on the disputed border with Afghanistan, dividing the Pashtuns. Hungary is building a second electrified wall to keep out migrant workers from Serbia and Croatia.

Walls are built not only to keep out the undesirables, but also to keep in the desirables. The Berlin Wall was built to stop the brain drain from East Germany crossing over to the West.

The most captivating walls are abstract and ideological. They are built within the populations, communities, and nations. These walls serve both to keep in and keep out individuals. A racial population may build a wall around itself through segregation, apartheid, and anti-miscegenation laws. A religious population may build a wall around itself through theology, self-righteousness, and laws against apostasy. Gated communities keep out the poor, the strangers, the loiterers, and even annoying guests.

Whether physical or ideological, a wall is essentially a contest of wills. It is a playable game. A wall furnishes an evanescent psychological comfort to the walled-ins. The same wall, however, ignites the audacious spirit of the walled-outs. Border guards armed with weapons, infrared cameras, drones, and all-terrain vehicles look for smugglers, terrorists, and plain old illegals. On the other side, the ecstasy of painting graffiti on the wall, climbing over the wall, drilling holes in the wall, and laying underground tunnels probe the wall's fragile impenetrability.

Contrary to the game plan of engineers and architects, all walls crumble one way or the other. Some walls age gracefully and turn into spectacular ruins. Some are opened to tourists for strolling. Some are erased to unify the divided cities. White women procreate with black men. Mexicans turn into patriotic Americans. Christians and Jews rescue besieged Muslims. The Iron Curtain has pulled apart. The Palestinian and IRA "terrorists" feast at the White House.

As always, much like demons in the darkness, even if you don't believe in evil spirits, Trumps, Wilders, Le Pens, and Al-Baghdadis are brewing rhetoric, cement, and concrete in cauldrons to shield the nation, the race, and the religion with high and mighty walls.

9 Profiling Islamophobes

Islamophobia in America is the fear and hatred of Islam and
Muslims prevailing among Christian and Jewish Americans.
(Atheists who question the very notion of religion are perhaps less
likely to select Islam as a special target of disparagement.) Most
American Christians and Jews do not fear or hate Islam or
Muslims. In fact, many Christian and Jewish interfaith
organizations are actively engaged in repelling Islamophobia.
American Jews understand that they too will be a prime target, as
recent cemetery vandalism and bomb threats demonstrate if
Islamophobia gains intensity and momentum. Likewise,
Mormons, Hindus, Sikhs, and other minority religious groups
living in America fear for their safety as the hatred of Islam sweeps
the nation.

The ugliest American Islamophobes that occupy prominent
social, political, and intellectual fields are well known to the world
if not to the people of the United States: They are Steve Bannon
(Irish Catholic), Robert Spencer (Greek Catholic), David Horowitz

(Jewish), Pamela Geller (Jewish), David Yerushalmi (Jewish), Frank Gaffney (Irish Catholic), Steven Emerson (unknown heritage), Daniel Pipes (Jewish), Sean Hannity (Irish Catholic), and Bill O'Reilly (Irish Catholic). There are scores of other Islamophobes, less highflying but no less vicious, firmly occupying posts in the media, legislatures, television, and academia.

These garrulous Islamophobes write books, sponsor seminars, and write op-eds; some prompt states to enact anti-Sharia legislation, some finance anti-Islamic political movements in Europe and the United States, some provide radio and television commentaries sensationalizing the perils of Islam, and some outright advocate the persecution and expulsion of American Muslims.

A quick overview of the ugliest Islamophobes listed above demonstrates that they are mostly white males, and mostly Irish Catholic or Jewish. It is ironic how these ugliest Islamophobes conveniently forget that Jews, Catholics, and the Irish — their own communities — have experienced sorrowful histories of discrimination, prejudice, hatred, and refusal to enter the United States. Anti-Semitism is the fear and hatred of the Jews. Hibernophobia is the fear and hatred of the Irish. It is a question of psychiatry, if not psychosis, why the descendants of the victims of Anti-Semitism and Hibernophobia have turned into malicious Islamophobes.

Profiling is inherently obnoxious and a questionable generalization from both moral and empirical viewpoints. Profiling is stereotyping, maybe carrying a trace of truth but almost always over-inclusive - a fishing net catching the blameless and the blameworthy. Stereotypes such as African-Americans are violent, Native-Americans are alcoholics, and Muslims are terrorists – all are odious and wrong. To this questionable list of stereotypes, I am in no hurry to add Irish Catholics and Jews as Islamophobes.

But I wonder. When Sean Hannity and Bill O'Reilly fume against Islam or Muslims with the intent to poison hearts and minds of the FOX viewers, do they ever simultaneously think about the Irish, the Catholic, or the Irish Catholic communities? When Daniel Pipes and David Horowitz intellectualize hatred against Islam and Muslims, do they ever simultaneously think about similar intellectualization of hatred against the European Jews who faced expulsion and extermination? At this point, in a free-flowing stream of consciousness, I am thinking of Ben Carson, an African-American, speaking in vivid delirium against Syrian refugees and discounting African slavery as a form of illegal immigration.

Producers of Islamophobia may be distinguished from consumers of Islamophobia. The producers are highly educated or highly powerful individuals, such as Steve Bannon. The individuals identified in this commentary are the producers of Islamophobia. For example, David Yerushalmi markets his Islamophobia to state legislatures, Sean Hannity to his television viewers. The consumers of Islamophobia are frequently less educated or less powerful, who can be easily swayed into hating Islam or Muslims. A person pulling the hijab off a Muslim woman walking down the street is a consumer of Islamophobia as is the person shooting "Iranians" (who were indeed Indians) in a Kansas bar. By every standard, the producers of hatred are worse foes of humanity than the consumers of hatred.

Over the centuries, Islamophobes have trashed Islam, persecuted and even killed Muslims. But there is a great irony in Islamic history. The Mongols destroyed Baghdad but their children embraced Islam. Even the Prophet's own uncle (Abu Lahb) was a vicious Islamophobe, and Mecca, now the citadel of Islam, was once an Islamophobic city. American Islamophobes, the ugliest and the less ugly, need to know that American Muslims and their progeny, even if persecuted, will continue to contribute to the economic, social, moral, and intellectual good of America as they have in Malaysia and Indonesia, nations as far away from the Middle East as are the United States.

10 Boomers' Last President

Demographics are unmistakable. Millennials (born after 1980) voted for Trump in far fewer numbers than did Boomers (born between 1946 and 1964). More than 53% Boomers voted for Trump but more than 55% Millennials voted against Trump. And millions of Millennials are less than 18 years old, who could not vote in the 2016 general elections. There are 120 million Millennials under 34, an emerging voting population that would change the dynamics of electoral politics.

As diversity-supportive Millennials replace diversity-skeptic Boomers, it will be almost impossible for men who denigrate women, racial and religious minorities, immigrants, and praise "good ole days" to win public trust. Trump is the last President of Boomers' America. Racial animus that has plagued America for centuries may eventually recede as Boomers, guarding the last citadel of old values, exit the scene and Millennials take over.

Of course, all Boomers cannot be labeled as backward-looking. (Broad generalizations are inherently inaccurate.) Millions of

Boomers as teachers, government officials, religious leaders, journalists, judges, workers, in numerous ways have made significant contributions to fighting for civil rights and fighting against social and economic inequality. They have tried to build a more generous America.

However, millions of Boomers continue to hold on to a fantasized version of America in which a white male aristocracy is identified with superior intellect, organizational skills, and leadership qualities. Boomers have been willing to make some room for women and non-whites provided the aristocracy hold on to the higher levels of power where important decisions are made. This view of the hierarchy has determined social and economic life, including government, sports, universities, and businesses.

Unfortunately, Boomers' formative consciousness was traumatic. As children and teenagers, Boomers watched a racially-torn America. They experienced the great social conflicts. They saw race riots while some parts of the country were under legal apartheid. They saw dogs and water hoses hounding black protesters.

They also witnessed revolutionary changes in America. In 1954, segregation was declared illegal, though it persisted for many years to come. In the 1960s, immigration was opened to non-whites. In 1963, the Supreme Court recognized a "constitutional" right to an attorney providing protection to defendants trapped in the criminal justice system. In 1966, Miranda warnings stemmed the powers of the law enforcement agencies. In 1967, the Supreme Court declared anti-miscegenation laws to be unconstitutional.

Boomers witnessed social forces pulling America out of darkness into the light of shared liberty. After achieving adulthood, millions of Boomers approved the changes but millions were resentful. The resentful millions, mostly living in rural America, got a new voice with Donald Trump (a Boomer). They wish to restore America to its "old grandeur." Steve Bannon, Michael Flynn, Jeff Sessions are the prime specimen of resentful Boomers.

History, much like a forceful river, cannot stay still. Millennials are replacing Boomers. The formative experiential basis of Millennials is a culturally diverse America. For them, the traditional white-black divide no longer captures the complexity of American social fabric. Vietnamese, Koreans, Somalis, North Africans, South Asians, and many other immigrant groups from all over the world have entered America. If Boomers saw a mostly white and black America, Millennials see a rainbow of races, ethnicities, and religions.

Thus, Millennials are the children of diversity. Their psychology is constructed differently. Millennials have no experience of race-based segregation in schools, buses, restaurants, and swimming pools. They are free to fall in love and marry across racial and gender boundaries. They see the world through the internet and Facebook, and not just local versions of America through local newspapers as did Boomers. There were hardly any mosques when Boomers were growing up in cities and small towns. For Millennials, Muslims and mosques are not exotic. For Boomers, the ownership of America lays exclusively in the hands of the white aristocracy. Millennials see no one group has a monopoly over key offices at the federal and state levels.

Millennials applauded when the Supreme Court overturned its prior ruling and declared the same-sex marriage as a constitutionally protected right. Millennials do not see Mexicans as intruders. They do not wish to rip off hijab from the face of Muslim women. Millennials cheered when the Supreme Court made it unlawful to discriminate against women wearing hijab. Protesting Trump's Executive Order to ban Muslims, Millennials crowded the U.S. airports, offering solidarity, comfort, and legal assistance.

Of course, Millennials are not immune from race relations that continue to generate social conflicts. Dylan Roof, who perpetrated the Charleston church massacre, is a Millennial. Richard Spencer, the white supremacist, lives on the cusp of being a Millennial. There will always be diversity-skeptic folks in America, including Millennials. No society is ever healed fully from its chronic ills.

Boomers will leave behind a mixed record and a controversial presidency of Donald Trump. There are verifiable clues that Millennials will not follow the psychology or white nationalism that the Trump team is advocating. Diversity will flourish in the decades to come and the alarmist notions of national security will lose credibility. The wall, if built by Boomers, may well be dismantled by Millennials. Millennials see the Muslim faith as part of American plurality. Trump presidency is the last show of Boomer's America, which the Millennials may or may not allow to be fully performed.

11 Trump is a Muslim

This is no spoof or fake news. President Donald J. Trump (J stands for Jumma, which means Friday in Arabic) is a Muslim who converted to Islam years ago, long before he challenged President Obama's birth certificate and faith credentials. Upon conversion, Trump was awarded the title of Sheikh, which means the scholar of Islam. Here are seven clues that President Trump is a practicing Muslim:

1. Sheikh Trump does not eat pork or consume alcohol. No Muslim, even if they skip prayers or fasting, eats pork. And the Shariah prohibits the consumption of all forms of alcohol (including Russian vodka). As a true Muslim, Sheikh Trump loathes bacon and sausages and has not touched alcohol in his life.

2. President Trump does not want to disclose his tax returns because for many years, actually, since his conversion to Islam, he has donated millions of dollars in charitable contributions to build mosques in the United States and around the world. Realizing that

voters are not ready to accept his faith credentials, Sheikh Trump wisely decided to withhold his tax returns from the public.

3. President Trump recruited numerous decoys in his cabinet to conceal his conversion to Islam. Too bad, Michael Flynn, who called Islam cancer, had to be fired. However, Steve Bannon and Stephen Miller are furnishing excellent camouflage. There are unsubstantiated rumors, though, that Steve has also converted to Islam to please his boss. If so, Sheikh Trump might have to hire yet another Islamophobe to throw sand in voters' eyes.

4. Sheikh Trump has a unique way of exposing the bigotry against Islam and Muslims, particularly in some parts of the United States. Out of his infinite wisdom, Sheikh Trump claimed that thousands of Muslims in New Jersey were cheering the collapse of the twin towers on 9/11. This story was a sarcastic exposure to how Muslims have been falsely blamed for supporting terrorism. Likewise, Sheikh Trump asked Kellyanne Conway to fabricate the massacre at Bowling Green to further show how Muslims can be easily blamed for fictitious terror attacks. A few days ago, Sheikh Trump himself invoked the non-existent "terrorist attack in Sweden" to continue to make the point that his Muslim brothers and sisters are systematically slandered.

5. Soon after occupying the White House, President Trump called the Saudi King to reaffirm his faith in Islam. He also called General Sisi of Egypt, President Erdogan of Turkey, and the prime minister of Pakistan to make sure they all understand that the travel ban on Muslims is just a ruse to please the deplorables. Trump asked his team to make an executive order that will not stand in a court of law and federal judges would unanimously declare it unenforceable. This executive order was a masterstroke

to fulfill a campaign promise, disguise the faith, and continue to allow fellow Muslims to pour into America. It is no wonder there were hardly any protests in any Muslim country against the travel ban.

6. On the day of inauguration, while President Obama and President-Elect Trump were scooting in the same limousine, Obama shared a secret with Trump. "Bring your ear close to my mouth," requested Obama. Trump did and what Trump heard was a low whisper: "Allah al Akbar" Trump winked his right eye, Obama his left, and they shared a hearty laughter.

7. On the day of inauguration, an unprecedented crowd of millions witnessed President Trump taking the oath on two holy books to uphold the constitution. Never in the history of the United States has a President used two copies of the same holy book to take the oath. Neither did Sheikh Trump. Given that Sheikh Trump is a very, very, very intelligent man he came up with the machination of using two holy books. Of course, one of the books was . .!

Over the weekend, Sheikh Trump attended the New York rally "I am a Muslim too" held in Time Square. Dishonest media and the failing NYT would never be able to figure out these clues. Clueless @realDonaldTrump

12 Threats of Deportation

Threats of deportations are evolving into a global phenomenon as nativism, racism, and xenophobia sweep the world. All over the world, nations are turning against "foreigners," particularly against the most vulnerable populations such as refugees, migrant workers, and undocumented immigrants. For example, Pakistan is forcing millions of Afghan refugees born in Pakistan to "go back home." Myanmar is persecuting the Rohingyas, an unwanted religious minority, pressing them to leave the country. Saudi Arabia has been expelling migrant workers after consuming their labor for years. Right-wing Europeans wish to oust even legal immigrants from North Africa, South Asia, and the Middle East. The United States has escalated its campaign to deport hundreds of thousands of undocumented immigrants.

This commentary focuses on the potential deportation of eleven (11) million undocumented immigrants, including six (6) million of Mexican national origin, the largest group of undocumented immigrants living in the United States. These immigrants live in mortal fear of the Immigration and Customs Enforcement (ICE) agents picking them up from work, school, home, hand-cuffing them, putting them in buses and planes, and discarding them out of a country they have made a home for years, if not decades. A Mexican man leaped off a bridge and killed himself after being deported. This cruel expulsion is justified under the popular label of "illegal aliens" and under the rhetoric of removing rapists and criminals.

International law in the form of human rights, international criminal law, the humanitarian law of war, regional compacts including the Charter on the Organization of American States, treaty provisions of state constitutions, and universal norms identified in scholarly treatises, all endorse, directly or indirectly, a simple principle that deportation is a crime against humanity.

The Nuremberg tribunals stated in unambiguous terms that enslavement or deportation of a population is a crime against the customary international law. *See* Robert Jackson, *The Nuremberg Case* xiv-xv (1971). Further, Nuremberg Principle IV(b) provides that the "deportation to slave labor ... of civilian populations of or in occupied territory" constitutes both a "war crime" and a "crime against humanity."

Building on the Nuremberg principles, more recent international treaties, and scholarly treatises reaffirm that deportation is a crime against humanity, even if committed in peace times, and even if the deported population is not shipped to slave labor. In addition to apartheid, disappearances, torture, and enslavement, Article 7 of the Rome Statute of the International Criminal Court lists deportation or forcible transfer of population as a crime against humanity. Article 4 of the 4th Protocol to the European Convention on Human rights states: "Collective expulsion of aliens is prohibited." In the United States, courts have reaffirmed the principle that deportation of civilian populations to slave labor is a crime.

Time is ripe for the US courts to reconsider the deportation of settled communities. This commentary offers the concept of adverse citizenship derived from the prohibition against deportation as a crime against humanity.

Several arguments may be offered to challenge the thesis that US deportation of undocumented immigrants is a crime against humanity. First, it might be argued that forced expulsion of only citizens/legal residents could be a crime against humanity and, therefore, the prohibition does not cover undocumented immigrants. Second, the United States is not a signatory to the Rome Statute or a party to the European Convention on Human Rights and the Protocols. Third, no US court has ruled that deportation of undocumented immigrants is contrary to the US Constitution, much less a crime against humanity. In fact, federal immigration laws allow deportation of undocumented immigrants and removal of some illegal aliens under expedited procedures. To cap these arguments, one might point out that if deportation of undocumented immigrants were to be a crime against humanity, nations will surrender their sovereignty to alien invaders.

These arguments have some merit under the US notion of sovereignty, as the distinction between legal and undocumented immigrants lays at the heart of US immigration law. *But see* The Extinction of Nation-States.

Yet, in the case of settled communities, the legal/illegal distinction is elusive, if not abusive to fundamental rights and liberties. With respect to undocumented communities, the US enforces its deportation laws in an arbitrary, cruel and unusual manner, in fits and starts, using the threat and actual removal as an instrument of mental torture, which itself is a crime against humanity.

The so-called undocumented immigrants in the United States are living in plain view of the federal government and enforcement agencies, including the Department of Homeland Security, Department of Justice, Congress, and the White House. They are not hiding in caves or mountains. They live and work in big cities and farming towns, in almost all states. Many speak their own native languages, and some undocumented immigrants speak not a word of English because they live in places that once belonged to Mexico and later conquered by the United States through wars. It is no secret that millions of undocumented immigrants have been residing in the United States for decades, giving birth to at least one, if not two, generation of US citizens.

The US itself is conflicted over the future of undocumented immigrants. In 2013, a bipartisan Senate bill proposed to provide a path to legal status for millions of undocumented immigrants on the theory (affirmed by the Congressional Budget Office) that such a path could reduce the deficit by $700 billion in 20 years. Some congressional bills instruct the Secretary of Homeland Security not to disclose the identity of undocumented immigrants brought as children to the ICE. Some proposed policies aimed at deporting only those undocumented immigrants who have committed crimes, and not others. Only extreme demagogues advocate removing all undocumented immigrants, a task that no one believes can be accomplished.

Settled communities with no documents acquire a right to "adverse citizenship' – a concept I offer for the courts to consider. Somewhat similar (though not exactly) to the common-law doctrine of adverse possession, it might be forcefully argued that undocumented immigrants living for years in the United States, paying taxes, and the federal government having full knowledge of their undocumented status, acquire a right to US citizenship. Such undocumented communities are no different from early colonists who entered America and acquired land and citizenship through adverse possession.

Regardless of legal origin, families and communities settled in various states have been participants in promoting the economy and welfare of the United States. A settled Mexican family is no different from a settled Scottish, Czechoslovakian, or Slovenian family. Uprooting settled families, separating children from parents, tearing apart spouses from each other, can no longer be defended under the prevailing norms of human dignity, equal protection, and due process. Deportation is a crime against humanity. Much like genocide, even deportation as part of an undocumented community is a crime against humanity. No notion of sovereignty may be asserted to defend wholesale or partial genocide, apartheid, disappearances, or deportations.

In 1986, President Ronald Reagan signed a law that allowed about four million undocumented immigrants to regularize their status. Since 1986, Congress has passed seven amnesty statutes to confer potential citizenship on undocumented immigrants. These amnesties are consistent with international law against deportation and support the concept of adverse citizenship.

President Trump's policy decision to deport undocumented immigrants is a crime against humanity, particularly with respect to families who have settled in the United States for long periods of time, have established homes, or have minor children. It is irrelevant whether these residents entered or stayed in the United States illegally. Deportation of a settled family or community is a violation of the right to life, right to family, right to property, right to privacy, and numerous other rights protected under customary international law, human rights treaties, due process, and fundamental legal principles that sustain the concept of law. If the US fails to enforce its immigration laws for years and allows families to lay their roots, the balance of equities shifts in favor of resident families to claim adverse citizenship. Through <u>laches</u>, the US loses its power to remove undocumented immigrants openly living, working, and paying taxes for decades.

13 Trapped in Afghanistan

Put aside the prognostic historical narratives that Afghanistan is the graveyard of invading superpowers. Based on concrete facts, analyzed below, the US faces a difficult future in Afghanistan and has two options: first, and the better one, leave Afghanistan as quickly as possible; second, stay and continue sacrificing American sons and daughters, recruited mostly from less privileged families. Because very few US politicians and policymakers send their own children to fight wars they advocate, they have no skin in the game and hence they are unlikely to propose leaving Afghanistan. Likewise, the military generals demanding more troops will rarely enter the battlefield staking their own bodies to enemy attack. Not to persuade but to caution the U.S. establishment occupying comfortable offices in Washington D.C., this commentary argues that the US has zero optionality of a military victory even though it can inflict manifold more devastation on the people of Afghanistan.

History often provides a justificatory context for starting a war and then vanishes in the background to witness nations trapped in armed conflict. In 2001, the U.S. had a credible, though unwise, basis to invade Afghanistan. Recall that the 9/11 terrorist attacks were allegedly perpetrated by Osama bin Laden operating under the protection of the Taliban government. Overthrowing the Taliban infrastructure and destroying Al-Qaeda justified the U.S. invasion. The NATO invoked Article 5 of its Charter to support the invasion. The UN Security Council "called upon the Member States to contribute personnel, equipment and other resources to the Force (U.S.)." The whole world descended on Afghanistan.

Yet, the Afghanistan war, much like a blurred movie, progressed to confuse the global audience. The Taliban were quickly overthrown and the Al-Qaeda was degraded with mega bombs. The NATO allies gradually departed, leaving the U.S. alone to face the tenacious Muslim militants. The U.S. started other wars in the Middle East but did not leave Afghanistan. Meanwhile, the Pashtuns in Pakistan started to assist their kinsfolks in Afghanistan and Pakistan too was inducted into the conflict, though not fully. Because of domestic complexities, Pakistan offered logistical support to the U.S. but refused to join the war. The U.S. has used carrots and sticks to bring Pakistan armed forces into the Afghan conflict but failed.

As a frustrated superpower, the U.S. disregards the obligation of laws. It resorts to torture in Afghan prison camps. On slightest suspicion, the U.S. Special Forces pick Afghan teachers and taxi drivers and transport them to Guantanamo. The erratic bombings hit wedding parties. The drone warfare is started to kill "terrorists" but innocent civilians are slaughtered. The U.S. loses its moral and legal justification to stay in Afghanistan. The 9/11 atrocities recede into archives, making room for U.S. war crimes. In the midst of U.S. wars in Iraq, Libya, and Syria, Afghanistan morphs into terminal poison for the occupying forces. Befuddled U.S presidents, one after the other, cannot disentangle the U.S. from Afghanistan. The regional powers make sure that the U.S. remains ensnared in an unwinnable war.

Slowly but steadily, like proverbial tortoises, the regional powers assemble to avenge their grievances against the United States. Without signing any treaty, without issuing any joint communique, and without forging any coordinated strategy, Iran, China, Russia, and Pakistan, all develop a shared interest in exposing the U.S. in Afghanistan to a thousand cuts, week after week.

For years, the U.S. has marked out Iran as the country that sponsors "international terrorism." U.S. sponsored economic sanctions strangle the Iranian standard of living. Iran has been looking for opportunities to get even with the U.S. For many years, Iran has soundlessly supported the Taliban and other regional militants to wound the U.S. forces operating in Afghanistan. Sharing a lengthy border with Afghanistan, Iran has unlimited optionality to reinforce the militants fighting the U.S.

China, perhaps the shrewdest country on the planet, has not sent armed forces to Afghanistan. Nor does China assist local militants with weapons. China employs the development card to unseat the U.S. from Afghanistan. The people of Afghanistan hear the message that while the U.S. is destroying their country in the name of liberty and democracy, China will improve their lives regardless of the form of government, including the Taliban rule. Strategically, China has every interest in seeing a fully disgraced U.S. bleed in Afghanistan.

In contradistinction to China, Russia has every reason to see the U.S. writhe, and suffer nakedly, in Afghanistan. The Russian support for the Afghan militants fighting the U.S. is extensive and unceasing. For Russia, the memories are still fresh how the United States unleashed "jihad" against the Soviet forces that occupied Afghanistan in 1979. Even if President Trump had reset the US-Russia relations, Russia could not have spared the opportunity to get even with the U.S. in the same battlefield, Afghanistan, where Russia was thoroughly humiliated. Russia is known to be unforgiving and revengeful.

Pakistan will play the most effective role in seeing that the U.S. is mired in Afghanistan, partly because the U.S. is divorcing Pakistan to marry India, a huge U.S. putdown for Pakistan's otherwise thoroughly pro-American ruling elites. Furthermore, Pakistan, now protected by China, will not enter the Afghan war under any U.S. pressure. Pakistan will allow its airspace and territory to be used for the influx of the U.S. forces and equipment into Afghanistan. Pakistan is the most convenient and the cheapest route for the U.S. access to Afghanistan. The U.S. will be forced to end its war in Afghanistan if Pakistan refuses to provide logistical resources. Pakistan will not close its airspace or territory for the U.S. forces primarily because Pakistan makes money for this service.

India, a budding U.S. ally in the region, also reaps economic and diplomatic benefits if the U.S. is jammed in a fruitless war in

Afghanistan. The U.S. establishment foolishly believes that India can counterbalance other regional powers. India has no will or ability to weaken the enclave of Iran, China, Russia, and Pakistan, each avenging its own grievances and pursuing national objectives. Most importantly, India does not care if the U.S. bleeds profusely in Afghanistan.

In sum, all regional powers, Iran, China, Russia, Pakistan, and India, crave for the U.S. to remain trapped in Afghanistan and face bloodbaths, in addition to burning billions of tax dollars. In this big geopolitical game, the U.S. has no chance of winning the war while the unfortunate Afghans will suffer huge losses for even more years to come.

14 Pakistan's Anti-Fragility

Pakistan thrives on disorder and adversity, pursuing Nassim Taleb's notion of antifragility. In India, Pakistan is bemoaned as a failed terrorist state. In Washington D.C., Pakistan is smeared as a duplicitous state, a posturing friend in the guise of a surreptitious foe. In Europe, Pakistan is hailed as one of the smartest countries in the world. In the Muslim world, Pakistan is acclaimed as a protective nuclear-state that would safeguard the holy cities of Makkah and Medina. Despite chronic energy shortage, Pakistan's stock market is a top performer in the world. Pakistan's cricket team has risen from slimy rigging scandals to win the 2017 international championship.

Pakistan, this land of Osama bin Laden and Malala Yousafzai, harbors both predators and preys with open hearts and a clear conscience, baffling rectilinear moralists, orthodox policymakers, and nations as strong as the United States.

The U.S. policymakers consistently fail to understand Pakistan's antifragility. For example, for over twenty years (1976-

1998), the U.S. made every effort to prevent Pakistan from developing the nuclear weapons technology. President Jimmy Carter used "carrots and sticks" to pressure Pakistan to abandon its nuclear program. On cues from Carter, Prime Minister Morarji Desai threatened to smash by force Pakistan's first nuclear bomb in the silo.

In 1979, the quantum mechanics of US-Pakistan entanglement shifted. When the Soviet Union invaded Afghanistan, President Carter offered a huge aid package to seek Pakistan's assistance, which Pakistan rejected as "peanuts." The U.S. had little option but to downsize its sticks and increase the quantum of carrots. When the price was right, Pakistan came on board to train the "freedom fighters" repelling the Soviet occupation.

On the nuclear issue, the U.S. Congress followed a legislative track to force Pakistan into submission. In 1985, Congress passed the Pressler Amendment to withhold military and economic assistance if Pakistan was found to be manufacturing a nuclear device. In 1998, Pakistan exploded six underground nuclear devices as a tit-for-tat reaction to the Indian nuclear tests. President Bill Clinton imposed economic sanctions under the 1994 Glenn Amendment and the 1961 Symington Amendment formulated to deter nuclear proliferation. Despite these sanctions, subsequent U.S. Presidents found ways to waive sanctions. In fact, Pakistan's antifragility improved even further.

In 2001, the 9/11 terrorist attacks deepened the U.S. entanglement with Pakistan. The U.S. could not invade Afghanistan, then the home of Al Qaeda, without Pakistani assistance. Shrewd Pakistan ditched the Taliban government and allowed its territory and airspace to be used for transporting the

U.S. military equipment and forces to invade Afghanistan. Thus, Pakistan mined a golden opportunity to have the economic sanctions lifted and furthermore have its nuclear-weapons recognized. The Pressler Amendment, the Glen Amendment, and the Symington Amendment, indeed the entire legislative track of economic sanctions fell flat on its nose. The U.S. money began to flow into Pakistan, like never before.

Now for more than fifteen years (2001-2017), the U.S. is fighting a failed war in Afghanistan, wasting billions of tax dollars. During this time, Pakistan has accelerated its nuclear weapons program, fast approaching the rank of a formidable nuclear power with efficacious short range and long-range delivery systems. Officially, Pakistan's nuclear defense rhetoric highlights possible attacks from India, but its nuclear program has profound international implications for Asia and the Middle East.

To further fortify its antifragility, Pakistan has initiated a chaotic political shift from military rule to democracy. Unlike Arab nations, Pakistan has realized that Muslim dictatorships (Saddam, Gadhafi, Assad, and Iranian theocracy) have been easy Western military targets and that electoral democracy (even if limited to a few families) is a better sociological and geopolitical defense against possible Western invasions.

When the U.S. policymakers and Congressmen visit Islamabad to complain about the Haqqani network operating from Pakistan, they confront a pack of *Aflatoons* (Platonic philosophers), some in military uniforms, some in pinstriped suits, and a few in *shalwar-kameez*, prattling hypotheses on the density and intractability of the Afghan conflict. These *Aflatoons* contend that the Americans see a clouded reality that deviates from the pure forms of understanding. After listening to softly-delivered Pakistani reservations against destroying the Haqqani network, the U.S. Senators return home saying ""If they don't change their behavior, maybe we should change our behavior towards Pakistan as a nation."

While the U.S. policymakers are still tied to the dysfunctional "carrots and sticks" policy toward Pakistan, the rise of China as a superpower has dramatically altered the geopolitical dynamics in the world, particularly South Asia. A deepening relationship between China and Pakistan, touted as "taller than the mountains and deeper than the oceans," is releasing Pakistan from the economic and military dependency on the U.S.

For Pakistan, shifting toward China has been an ascending hypotenuse. China is a contiguous neighboring state while the U.S. is a distant outsider. China has veto power in the Security Council to protect Pakistan from any India-prompted or Western coordinated aggressive policy. For example, China blocks resolutions in the UN Sanctions Committee to ban Pakistani "terrorist groups" tormenting India. Most importantly, China is able and willing to spend loads of money in Pakistan that the U.S could never do.

Yet Pakistan woos the U.S. as a potential ally. This is a remarkable piece of geopolitical antifragility. Pakistan does not think in binary terms. Picking either the U.S. or China is never a serious option. After the 9/11 attacks, President George W. Bush's unforgettable command "you're either with us or against us" was principally aimed at Pakistan. Pakistan heard the command, sided with the U.S. in the invasion of Afghanistan, but quickly backtracked to its non-binary mindset.

Pakistan provides logistical support to the U.S. armed forces but stubbornly refuses to fight the American war in Afghanistan. This indeed is the Haqqani network paradox.

Now, China, Pakistan, Russia, and the Taliban are determined to force the U.S. out of Afghanistan. The U.S. is relying on India's Modi to beat the odds of the Taliban regaining control of Afghanistan. Unfortunately, India cannot deliver what the U.S. needs in Afghanistan – a victory.

While the Afghanistan war lingers, the Chinese diplomats and government executives visit Islamabad and meet the *Aflatoons*. The ambiguity, the complexity, and the intractability that the Americans routinely face in Pakistan, all disappear leaving behind a clear-headed Confucian aphorism that the relationship is superior to transactions. In all these Chinese visits, Pakistan declares its unwavering commitment to the notion of One China, reaffirms China's sovereignty over the South China Sea, and offers complete control of the Gwadar seaport for transporting the Chinese goods to Africa and the Middle East.

Amid the chaos, political upheavals, energy shortage, domestic terrorism, and cross-border firings with India, Pakistan disregards the U.S. Pavlovian strategy of behavior modification and reinforces its own antifragility.

15 Nations Threatening the World

The weapons of mass destruction (WMD) come in three forms, nuclear weapons, biological weapons including toxins, and chemical weapons. Three global treaties prohibit the development and production of the WMD: Nuclear Non-Proliferation Treaty (NPT, 1970), Biological Weapons Convention (BWC, 1975), and Chemical Weapons Convention (CWC, 1977). The 1970s was a valuable decade for beginning the process of eliminating the WMD. Over the years, some nations have been reluctant to ratify the WMD treaties.

As of May 1, 2017, out of a total of 195 nation-states in the world, 191 are parties to the NPT, 178 are parties to the BWC, and 192 are parties to the CWC. The BWC is the least subscribed WMD treaty and efforts are underway to bring more nations into its prohibitive orbit.

Ratification and accession bind a nation-state fully under a treaty whereas mere signing a treaty imposes some obligations not to defeat the object and purpose of the treaty. International law does not require the two-step process of signing and ratifying treaties. Nations may directly ratify (called accession) a treaty without first signing it. For example, China ratified the BWC in 1984 without first signing it. Here I use the word ratification to include accession as well.

Nations that have not ratified the NPT are India, Pakistan, Israel, and North Korea. Nations that have not ratified the CWC are Egypt, Israel, and North Korea. And nations that have not ratified the BWC include Syria, Israel, and North Korea.

Thus, North Korea and Israel are the only two states that have not ratified any of the three WMD treaties. North Korea has not signed any of the three treaties whereas Israel has signed the CWC but not ratified it. In the absence of international inspections, the quantity and lethality of the WMD in possession of a non-signatory state is only a matter of conjecture.

North Korea is the most outlier nation as it has shown no commitment to reject the weapons of mass destruction. Furthermore, the political system of North Korea is highly dictatorial with an irremovable leader at the top. Even highly centralized dictatorships may have internal consultation processes and may even display wisdom in foreign policy. Yet the world feels threatened with dictators commanding the WMD.

In fact, a political dictatorship with an irremovable leader at the top undermines the value of ratification of the WMD treaties. For example, Iran has ratified all the WMD treaties. Yet, many nations and international organizations, including the UN Security Council, have been skeptical about the Iranian commitment to the NPT. Likewise, though Syria signed the CWC in 2013, the accusations that the Syrian government used chemical weapons in April 2017 seem credible because President Bashar Assad is an irremovable ruler.

In 2003, the US invasion of Iraq was defended on the fabricated pretext that Saddam Hussein, a brutal dictator, had been secretly developing nuclear weapons even though Iraq had ratified the NPT in 1969. Moreover, though Iraq had ratified the CWC in 1991, the charges that Iraq used chemical weapons against the Kurds were credible. Saddam's despotism devalued Iraq's ratification of the NPT and the CWC. In 2009, three years after the execution of Saddam, Iraq ratified the BWC.

It appears that the world is willing to tolerate the WMD in the possession of democratic nations. India and Pakistan have not signed or ratified the NPT, even though both are parties to the CWC and BWC. In 1998, India and Pakistan conducted nuclear tests in a tit-for-tat pattern. As compared to Pakistan, India's nuclear program is much more acceptable to the world and many nations are willing to endorse India for a permanent seat in the UN Security Council. This is so because India has demonstrated a solid commitment to democracy whereas Pakistan's democracy has remained unpredictable and prone to military takeovers. General Pervez Musharraf roams freely in the world while Pakistan's judicial system has been unable to prosecute him for his well-documented crimes against democracy. If Pakistan's democracy is overthrown again, a case might be made for the de-nuclearization of Pakistan.

Likewise, the world is extremely nervous about North Korea but less so about Israel even though both nations are similar in their non-adherence to the WMD treaties. Israel has been a democracy, though the world is critical of Israel's occupation of and settlements in the Palestinian territories.

The ideal setup for a peaceful world envisages democratic nations that have ratified all the WMD treaties. Even a better world is conceivable. Given the historically-evidenced inclinations of the human species toward destruction, a better world without the WMD remains an elusive but a worthwhile ambition.

16 Arab Rulers Detest Free Speech

Arab rulers across the Middle East detest free speech. The demand that Al- Jazeera close its operations is no surprise. Al-Jazeera (which means the island) offers talk shows, documentaries, and news in Arabic, the language of the region that reaches more than 350 million Arabic-speaking people from Mauritania to Yemen. Headquartered in Doha, Qatar, a native Arab land, Al-Jazeera has adopted an iconoclastic motto "opinion and the other opinion."

For most Arab rulers, there is always only one opinion, the opinion of the government, and for them, all other opinions are false, alien, and subversive. This commentary analyzes why Arab rulers are hostile to free speech, particularly the home-grown free speech, emanating from within the region, in Arabic dialects and metaphors, by Arab intellectuals, analysts, and critics.

For centuries, the Arab rulers are used to reverence, hand-kissing, and bowing. The Arab rulers, be they military officers, kings, emirs, or presidents, share a similar concept of leadership. They truly believe in their hearts that they are the men-in-authority chosen with the divine will. They cherish an automatically presumed self-concept of being noble, just, and sagacious. Witness how General Abdel Fattah al-Sisi, the Egyptian martinet, who overthrew a democratically-elected government, smiles with condescending wisdom. Such men as sovereigns (and there are no women Arab rulers) are not open to free speech.

Also, historically, the Arab rulers have been tolerant of foreign criticism but not of internal dissent. Even today, the Arab rulers tolerate the non-Arab opinions broadcasted by the BBC, Voice of America, Press TV (Iran), or any other foreign outfit because the Arab rulers rely on an overarching paradigm that the foreigners, including Europeans, Americans, and Iranians, brood ill-will against the glorious Arab civilization that once dominated the world for centuries and gifted the world with the religion of Islam. They dismiss the Europeans as colonists, they deride the Americans as Islamophobes, and they scorn the Iranians as Shias, who are corrupting the true message of Islam that only the Arab rulers understand and have been ordained by Allah to preserve.

Al-Jazeera offers internal dissent, which is interpreted as *baghyan* (rebellion). The real-time reporting that deviates from the official truth, the "unfavorable" documentaries, and intellectual ruminations, aired in various shows at Al-Jazeera, all are an internal threat to a political order that the Arab governments have imposed without the will of the people. Unintendedly, for that is the fallout of free speech, Al-Jazeera challenges the historical narrative of infallible Muslim rulers who can do no wrong.

In Arab countries, banning Al-Jazeera is seen as the right thing to suppress *fitna* (mischief), another convenient concept that the Arab rulers frequently invoke to arrest journalists, lash critics in public, and execute intellectuals and scholars. In Egypt, for example, Hassan al-Banna was assassinated in 1949, Sayyid Qutub was hanged in 1966, as both scholars were seen as the purveyors of *fitna*. President Morsi, elected in 2012, is in prison accused of terrorism and faces capital punishment. Egypt, the most prominent Arabic speaking country, has blocked or banned Al-Jazeera in cahoots with U.A.E, and Saudi Arabia. They all are determined to eliminate *fitna* (fake news, lies, and terrorism) that Al-Jazeera allegedly promotes.

The Arab rulers, the self-appointed defenders of "true religion," defame Islam as the peoples of the world gather the impression that Islam is hostile to democracy and free speech. Even though the majority of Muslims, living in Indonesia, Turkey, Iran, India, Pakistan, and many other nations, are non-Arabs, the world continues to associate Islam with the Arabs, particularly with Saudi Arabia, where the prophet is buried and where the Qur'an was revealed in Arabic. Despite the expansion of Islam in all continents, what the Arab rulers do or say have a significant bearing on the image of Islam for non-Muslims.

Even Islamophobia in the West is a distorted reaction to the Middle Eastern customs that have little to do with the teachings of Islam. Seeing that women cannot drive in Saudi Arabia, seeing that the leaders of Al-Qaeda and Islamic State hailed from Saudi Arabia, Egypt, and Iraq, and seeing the failed efforts to bring democracy in Arab countries, non-Muslims of the world construct a view of Islam rooted in misogyny, terrorism, and tyranny. The opposition to Shariah in the United States has everything to do with what the Americans witness in the Middle East.

Outside the Middle East, Islam has a different ethos. Consider Pakistan, a country carved out of India in the name of Islam. Only a few days ago, the Supreme Court disqualified a democratically elected prime minister, the highest political office in the country—an unthinkable event in the Arab heartland. In Pakistan, hundreds of newspapers and TV channels are determined on a daily basis to find faults with every aspect of the government and opposition. Although Pakistan has suffered military interventions, free speech has remained vibrant for most of its history. In this country, no credible paradigm paints the ruler as noble, wise, or appointed by Allah. Rulers are seen fallible and replaceable. Sometimes, the military generals get away with murder but this impunity is never associated with the dictates of Islam. In fact, even supporters of military generals advocate equality under the norms of Islamic justice.

Arab rulers detest free speech because they obtain and retain political power without the will of the people. They see free speech as a threat to the unrepresentative form of government they institute. The convenient labels of *baghyan* and *fitna*, mentioned in the Qur'an, are arbitrarily invoked to suppress legitimate criticism and dissent. The label of terrorism is also convenient to eliminate opposing viewpoints. The proposal to shut down Al-Jazeera reflects how the Arab rulers build their castles in the sand that cannot tolerate the winds of free speech.

17 Kill and Cure Strategy

On August 21, 2017, President Trump prescribed a new kill and cure medicine for winning the war in Afghanistan. Killing terrorists is the "kill part" of the medicine while negotiating with the Taliban at some surprise moment in the future is the "cure part." The kill part is not new. Since 9/11, U.S. presidents have employed soaring rhetoric to sell the kill part. President Bush executed the kill part through the invasions of Afghanistan and Iraq. President Obama, the recipient of the 2009 Nobel Peace Prize, staged drone strikes in Afghanistan, Pakistan, Somalia, and Yemen to kill both alien and citizen terrorists.

The "cure part" is sort of new because previously (even before 9/11) the U.S. presidents publicly vowed not to talk to the terrorists, though first secretly or sometimes openly, they all have negotiated with the leaders of terrorist organizations, including Yasser Arafat, Gerry Adams, Osama bin Laden, and Mullah Omar. Trump is simply making the cure part a bit less covert.

Killing "terrorists" is now a global practice of warfare that many nation-states endorse and act upon, ignoring the strictures of extra-judicial killings. Israel pioneered the state practice by killing Palestinian leaders in occupied territories, including the 2004 drone assassination of Sheikh Yassin, a quadriplegic leader of Hamas. Upon 9/11, the U.S. too adopted an open policy of killing terrorists. Recall, however, that the covert policy of killing foreign leaders has been for decades a part of the U.S. foreign policy.

The U.S. changed the kill rule of international law. When a minor state violates a rule of international law, it is considered a breach or crime; and, the violating state may be punished with economic sanctions or use of force. When a superpower violates a rule of international law, the rule itself loses legitimacy and may be abandoned if extensively violated. Such de-enactments of rules, though uncommon, are part of international lawmaking. Killing terrorists has been established as a recognized exception to the prohibition against extra-judicial killings.

One problem with the kill rule is the classification of terrorists subject to assassination. However, the classification is no longer confined to persons who personally commit acts of terrorism. A mastermind such as Osama bin Laden who finances terrorism is a legitimate target. So is an intellectual who incites resistance, as did Anwar Awlaki, a U.S. Citizen killed in a drone strike in Yemen. So is a spiritual leader, such as Sheikh Yassin. Afghan Taliban Chief Mullah Omar, though not killed, died under a hanging sword of U.S. bounty of $25 million placed on his head.

Theoretically, the kill part of the medicine may unleash fierce bombings of the Afghan Taliban who control the significant territory of Afghanistan. Mega bombs may be routinized in all parts of Afghanistan. Likewise, drone warfare may escalate both in Afghanistan and Pakistan. This course of chemotherapy, however, is highly improbable, despite the anticipation of medicine.

Even though Trump indicated that the U.S. is open to talking to some elements of the Taliban, the pragmatics will dictate that the U.S. negotiate with the Taliban leadership.

It is unclear how Pakistan would react to increased drone strikes within Pakistan. Previous U.S. administrations would use drones or other strikes, including the killing of Osama bin Laden, with permission from and prior notice to the Pakistan armed forces. This covert strategy is unlikely to change, though the public rhetoric from both governments may turn mutually antagonistic.

If perchance the Trump administration pursues a unilateral kill policy in Pakistan, the Afghanistan war will break for the worse. Pakistan may shoot down U.S. drones, cutoff supply routes, or unleash groups willing to fight India in Kashmir. This development will generate a head-on collision between Pakistan and the U.S. It is highly doubtful that the U.S. and Pakistan will resort to such extremity, given the close relationship between U.S. and Pakistan militaries and intelligence communities.

In sum, the kill part of the medicine will remain a tool of propaganda, though a lot of civilians will be killed in showoff bombings and drone strikes. Afghanistan, one of the poorest countries in the world, will continue to suffer adversity, as it has in the past. The U.S. will fail to eliminate the Taliban, strengthen Afghan democracy, or bring prosperity to the people of Afghanistan. The kill part will be downright ineffective.

By contrast, the cure part carries some promise. Trump made two things clear: first, the U.S. is no longer interested in nation-building or promoting democracy in Afghanistan. This means that the people of Afghanistan may choose a form of government other than liberal democracy or democracy at all. It also means that the people of Afghanistan may choose a form of government consistent with the Shariah principles, much like the people of Saudi Arabia or the United Arab Emirates. This ideological flexibility may pave the way for the Taliban to take interest in negotiating an exit deal with the U.S.

When a superpower violates a rule of international law, the rule itself loses legitimacy and may be abandoned if extensively violated.

The second thing that Trump made clear is the U.S. willingness to negotiate with the Taliban. Even though Trump indicated that the U.S. is open to talking to some elements of the Taliban, the pragmatics will dictate that the U.S. negotiate with the Taliban leadership. The cure part also means that Pakistan, commanding influence over the Afghan Taliban, will play a crucial role in shaping the future of Afghanistan. Pakistan furnishes the medium, the credibility, and the logistics for direct negotiation between the U.S. and the Afghan Taliban. To balance these services from Pakistan, Trump asks India to furnish resources for development in Afghanistan.

The U.S. can kill thousands of people in Afghanistan, as it has in the past sixteen years, but the kill medicine will not furnish a face-saving exit from this longest war in the U.S. history. The war will become ghastlier and the world less safe if the U.S. picks an unnecessary fight with Pakistan because Pakistan will divert its frustration against India, triggering yet another South Asian war. The way forward for the U.S. is no other but direct negotiation with the Taliban leadership without killing their leaders. Moreover, the time for negotiation is now and not at some unannounced surprise party in the future.

18 Trump on Pakistan

A confident Pakistan rejects President Trump's Afghanistan policy point by point. Pakistan argues: (1) while losing a fruitless war in Afghanistan, the U.S. needs Pakistan as a scapegoat to externalize its policy failures. The Haqqani network is not the prime reason for the U.S. military defeat; (2) the "billions and billions of dollars" the U.S. claims to have delivered to Pakistan are inadequate reimbursements for the military and infrastructural services that Pakistan has furnished over a period of sixteen years since the invasion of Afghanistan in 2001.

To further dispute Trump's contentions, Pakistan claims that it has suffered more than $100 billion in economic losses due to the U.S. invasion of Afghanistan since Pervez Musharraf's decision to support the invasion brought terrorism to Pakistan, preventing foreign investments and domestic development projects. These losses are heavier than any financial assistance the U.S. delivered to Pakistan. This argument implies that the U.S., rather than helping, has utilized Pakistan's resources and has been a net beneficiary.

Pakistan also points out that its military has suffered more losses than the U.S. military in terms of deaths and injuries to the soldiers. In 2015, the International Physicians for the Prevention of Nuclear War reported that more than 80,000 Pakistanis have been killed in the U.S. war on terror, including civilians and journalists. International studies support a higher death toll as the war grinds on and the militants refuse to surrender.

Even though Pakistan's economic and life losses due to the U.S. invasion of Afghanistan are significant, Pakistan must pause before it opts for ingratitude. Pakistan cannot deny the fact that the U.S. has been an ally and partner since the creation of Pakistan in 1947. For seventy years, the U.S. has furnished financial and technical assistance to Pakistan in agriculture, education, defense, international relations, and even in fighting the prior wars with India. Numerous Pakistani generals are trained in the United States. The U.S. import policy has been anything but favorable to Pakistani goods. For decades, the U.S. has exercised its superpower influence in the International Monetary Fund and the World Bank to facilitate crucial financial assistance to Pakistan.

Being ungrateful to the U.S. is not in the interest of Pakistan. Pakistan has close ties with the Anglo countries, including the United Kingdom, Canada, and Australia. Millions of Pakistanis work in these countries and remit hard currency to their families back home. If Pakistan breaks up with the U.S., the Anglo countries, which coordinate their foreign policy more intensely than the European Union, will not be kind to Pakistan. Similarly, the Gulf States, closely associated with the U.S., where millions of

Pakistani blue-collar workers migrate to support their families, will be under pressure to punish an ungrateful Pakistan one way or the other. Without remittances, Pakistan will be bankrupt in hard currency.

A rational Pakistan cannot be ungrateful to the U.S. However, the Trump presidency is a challenge that Pakistan needs to face with fortitude.

The U.S. is dramatically changing under the Trump presidency. Trump enjoys quarreling with individuals, groups, institutions, and nations — be it Australia, Mexico, or Pakistan. He loves to intimidate real and imagined adversaries (see Hillary Clinton). Pakistan should interpret Trump allegations in a broader context of his modus operandi.

Unfortunately, President Trump continues to act as if he is still a realtor in the rough world of contractors. He believes in getting a good deal out of first bullying and then giving concessions as a generous gift. First rattle and then gratify is the Trump formulary for dealing with everyone in the world, including Pakistan. Pakistan needs to take Trump speeches with a grain of salt.

Even more important is the fact that the U.S. diplomats are not the same as the feisty White House staff. Whatever the U.S. envoys and diplomats might say publicly or in private meetings, they are much more sophisticated and knowledgeable than the opponents might guess. The U.S. officials dealing with Pakistan know that Pakistan has been a faithful ally without a backbone and that in the past years Pakistan has accepted all conditions placed on the table. This image has been Pakistan's laughable negotiating tactic. Pakistan may rightfully develop a new negotiating model. Bullying aside, the U.S. generals and diplomats are fully aware of Pakistan's difficult domestic politics, complex demographics, porous borders, conflict with India, friendship with China, and civilian-military relations in Islamabad.

Furthermore, the U.S. comes across as a tough superpower, arrogant, self-obsessed, disregarding, and using other nations as mere dispensable tools in the non-quenching thirst for hegemony. Beneath this perception, the U.S. diplomatic culture is much softer and fair-minded. The U.S. values loyalty, friendship, trustworthiness, just as most nations do. International relations are no different than personal relations. After all, it is the same human species forming alliances.

Pakistan needs to pause and rethink its options. International relations are frequently portrayed as the ever-shifting pursuit of national interests. And the U.S. is painted as a selfish, predatory hegemon. However, this pejorative model does not explain the more complex reality of global politics or the U.S. mindset. Loyalty, gratitude, and sacrifice are strong values even in international relations. Pakistan and the U.S. have been allies for seventy years. They cannot walk away from each other by picturing a relationship of accusations, duplicity, betrayal, and exploitation. Trump's negotiating intimidation should not be an excuse for Pakistan to show ingratitude for many good things the U.S. has done for Pakistan. A patient and well-constructed argument for what Pakistan thinks must happen in Afghanistan is the way forward for stabilizing a rattled relationship with the U.S.

19 Monetization of International Relations

"**The point is** that you can't be too greedy." The author of this saying, President Trump, is brazenly monetizing international relations. He demands more money from the NATO members for the common defense. He urges Mexico to pay for the wall. He is slashing financial assistance to allies (except Israel). He vies to renegotiate trade agreements. He proposes to impose tariffs on Mexican and Canadian goods in violation of international trade laws. He campaigned in the 2016 presidential election to declare China as a currency manipulator. Much like a Las Vegas tycoon, Trump views the world as a big casino where the U.S. is losing money. Trump fancies rigging the international game for the U.S. to come out as a tireless winner.

Trump's money obsessions add nothing innovative to international relations. For centuries, money has been a dominant factor in relations among states. Occupations, invasions, war booty, indentured labor, and slavery were the common instruments for wealth aggregation. Now, nations marshal affluence through trade, investments, remittances, immigration, and migrant workers. Nations that have little to sell in international markets are poor. Nations with natural resources are vulnerable to subjugation. Nations raise huge armies and some develop weapons of mass destruction to commit as well as deter aggression. Predatory nations are armed to the teeth. Most nations are terrified. Fear rules the humankind.

By making money calls, Trump aggravates the undercurrents of self-interest permeating international politics. In many parts of the world, nations are terrorizing each other, seizing land and resources, seeking unfair advantage, spilling blood, and doggedly retarding the models of civilization that poets, philosophers, environmentalists, and ethicists romanticize. Trump is not an idealist. He is a coarse money merchant with little interest in the welfare of global civilization. Trump speaks the language of intimidation to defend and extort money. Millions of Americans detest Trump the man and Trump the money maniac.

Superpowers have action choices. A superpower can act as a greedy nation determined to aggregate wealth through exploitation, intimidation, threats, invasion, and occupation. It can also act as a benevolent world leader imbued with generosity, idealism, and wellbeing of all the peoples of the world. Sadly, most superpowers, including the British and Spanish colonial empires, have committed immense crimes against humanity, including massacres, theft of land, destruction of occupied cultures, and transfer of wealth from abroad to national exchequers.

As a superpower, the U.S. has been inconstant as it swings from one choice to the other. Reconstructing a war-ravaged Europe, financially supporting international organizations for peace and security, opening its borders for the poor and the tired of the world, and giving money for the prevention and elimination of epidemics in different parts of the world, these and other munificent acts make the United States a special superpower, one that endears the hearts of the world and inspires other nations to do good as a purposeful policy preference.

Trump contemplates the other choice, much like Spanish conquistadors and British imperial viceroys known for their treachery and gold-grabbing. Trump's affection for President Andrew Jackson, who stole millions of acres of land from Native Americans, reveals his predatory mindset. Trump's campaign utterings that the U.S. "should have kept the Iraqi oil" reinforce his deep-seated hunger to loot assets that belong to others. If Trump is allowed freely to shape international relations after his own mind, the U.S. will become a superpower that the peoples of the world would hate from the bottoms of their hearts.

What Trump misses to understand is the inherent will of other nations and communities to resist the dynamics of overreaching. If Trump opts for monetized national interests, other nations are unlikely to play dead. History demonstrates that Germany can be pushed only too far before it reacts with irrational might. So is Japan. Vietnam proved that a small nation resolved to defend itself can successfully fight a weighty war machine. Mexico refuses to succumb to Trump's monetized pressure, as does Iran, China, Venezuela, and Russia.

Of course, a superpower can determine the dynamics of world affairs. Nations tend to imitate superpowers, at least in dealing with superpowers. If Trump transforms the U.S. into a money-aggregating hegemon, the world is bound to resist and frustrate any such efforts. Turning selfish is not an act of genius for persons or nations. It's easy. The U.S. has no special privilege to be selfish. Yes, the U.S. may pursue its monetized self-interest with the use of force, including the weapons of mass destruction, but even this option is a loser rather than a winner. North Korea trapped tightly in economic sanctions, and facing starvation of its people, may be condemned as a crazy country but crazy countries do emerge in a world where superpowers terminate fair play in favor of dog-eat-dog imperative.

20 Showing Eyes to Trump

Ever since President Trump singled out Pakistan as the primary reason for the U.S. failure in Afghanistan, Pakistan has been "showing eyes" (آنکهیں دکھا نا) like never before. Historically, Pakistan has been timid and obsequious -- but not anymore. "Showing eyes" is an idiom in several South Asian languages, including Hindi, Punjabi, and Urdu. Showing eyes is a look, a scowl, a stare that radiates confrontational, rude, and contemptuous annoyance. John Steinbeck came close in capturing the meaning of showing eyes, when he wrote: "I've seen a look in dogs' eyes, a quickly vanishing look of amazed contempt, and I am convinced that basically dogs think humans are nuts."

Showing eyes is a more persistent deportment and not just a quickly vanishing disdain. For example, Pakistan has trimmed down its lavish protocols once reserved for the U.S. officials. Gone are the days when a junior state department officer could demand seeing the Pakistan prime minister. Gone are the days when the

U.S. senators were greeted with sumptuous dinners, flattering conversations, and unlimited access to civil and military top brass.

Pakistan's foreign minister tells a story of meeting with National Security Advisor General McMaster in Washington D.C. Minutes after entering the conference room, the General says to the foreign minister: "We have very minimal trust in Pakistan." The defiant foreign minister, known for his abrasive retorts, responds, "General, you should also know that Pakistan has zero trust in the United States." This exchange captures the essence of showing eyes.

Nothing exasperates Pakistan more than when another country, be it Iran, Afghanistan, or the U.S., ditches Pakistan to woo India. The Trump administration has been affirming the Indian policy of painting Pakistan as the mother of international terrorism. While the U.S. bleeds in a defiant Afghanistan and India in a resurgent Kashmir, both have a shared interest in scapegoating Pakistan as the surreptitious villain.

In 2001, Pakistan, as a recipient of civil and military assistance, had no choice but to support the U.S. invasion of Afghanistan. At the same time, however, Pakistan could not bluntly ignore the powerful domestic religious forces that advocate jihad against anti-Islamic nations. Short of fighting on the side of the U.S. military, Pakistan argues that it has delivered all possible assistance. Pakistan yielded its airstrips for flying the CIA drones in the region, allowed its roads and ports to be used for the movement of U.S. military hardware, and shared indispensable intelligence that resulted in the killing of numerous Afghans fighting the occupying forces in Afghanistan.

President Trump, it seems, is willing to see Pakistan dismantled - and that indeed is a major shift in the U.S. policy toward South Asia.

Muslim militants across the world, from Somalia to Yemen to Iraq to Afghanistan to Pakistan, share a common conviction that the U.S. is an anti-Islamic superpower. When they see Pakistan supporting the U.S. invasion forces, they divert their wrath against the civil and military targets, abundantly available throughout Pakistan. Pakistan cannot openly fight the militants because that means an unending civil war, no different than the one in Iraq or Syria.

By supporting the U.S. invasion of Afghanistan, therefore, Pakistan opted for pretense and double-dealing. Pakistan ran with the hare and hunted with the hounds. Even the killing of Osama bin Laden could not have occurred without the support of Pakistan high command that played deaf and dumb while the raid was taking place in Abbottabad. President Obama, who ordered Osama's assassination, knew that Pakistan simply could not own the U.S. military operation. The narrative that Pakistan was hiding Osama was deemed more palatable to the people of Pakistan than the account that Pakistan helped the U.S. in assassinating Osama bin Laden.

For decades, the U.S. policymakers have counted into the foreign policy calculus that Pakistan is made in the name of Islam and it cannot survive if Islam loses its unifying authority. They know that Pakistan is an ungovernable nation of historically discrete ethnic populations yoked together with the ideology of Islam. Some U.S. presidents understand this historical constraint more than others. Presidents Clinton, Bush, and Obama, while tilting toward India, worked under the historical constraint. President Trump, it seems, is willing to see Pakistan dismantled - and that indeed is a major shift in the U.S. policy toward South Asia.

Pakistan calculated its options for survival and chose to shift completely toward China. China, a neighbor to both India and Pakistan, trusts vulnerable Pakistan as a more reliable ally than relatively stronger India who has had territorial disputes with China. With restive Muslim minority of Uyghurs in Xinjiang, but no sizable Hindu population in China, China-Pakistan friendship makes credible geopolitical sense. Furthermore, China comes across as a pro-Islamic superpower as its leadership rarely makes anti-Islamic statements as do policymakers in the Trump administration.

Pakistan's showing eyes to the U.S. underscores a major development in international affairs. First, Pakistan is no longer an obsequious U.S. ally. Pakistan now insists on working with the U.S. based on equal respect and dignity. Second, the U.S. has fewer reservations if Pakistan falls apart as it would make a strong case for the denuclearization of Pakistan, a scenario many nations might welcome. Third, China will not allow Pakistan to be dismembered and the China-Pakistan alliance is likely to grow "taller than the mountains and deeper than the oceans," a piece of rhetoric that both countries repeatedly extemporize in various other forms.

21 The Merchant of Weapons

President Trump has turned into a merchant of weapons, coaxing nations to buy American weapons and warfare systems. Inevitably, modern U.S. presidents are obligated to support the manufacturers of warfare systems. The Republican presidents do it openly whereas the Democratic presidents do it through deceptive quietude. Trump has been most assertive in his rambunctious ways to push the sale of lethal weapons. (Recall how Trump, the realtor, boasts fooling Libya's Gadhafi by overcharging him for pitching a tent on Trump's New York City estate.) The U.S. warfare establishment sees war as a necessary evil that must always remain the prime factor in foreign policy.

The U.S. warfare establishment comprised of the Pentagon, CIA, White House, warfare industry and their lobbyists, imperial think-tanks (Heritage Foundation), warmongering theoreticians, and "hawkish" congressmen in the House and the Senate, all stimulate a culture of domestic and global fear to promote the making and vending of deadly weapons. Now for years, the war on terror has been used as a grand ploy less to fight the poorly-armed Muslim militants and more to hype the need for the nations' "self-defense "translated into the purchase of military aircrafts, missiles, bombs, tanks, and cyber warfare equipment.

The U.S. "defense" industry, an aggregation of hundreds of large and small companies, is a formidable juggernaut and part of the warfare establishment. It benefits when the establishment germinates, exasperates, and maintains potential and real wars across the globe.

The first victims of the warfare establishment are the American taxpayers, forced to disburse their hard-earned money to the Pentagon, a military hegemon that fritters away over $600 billion every year. The U.S. spends at least 20% of federal revenues on the military (whereas the education budget is less than 2%). On huge profits and soaring stocks, the top five companies in the warfare industry have multiplied their market capitalization by over 200%.

The U.S. warfare establishment adores Trump as a grandfatherly salesman to sell arms to a legion of countries, including Saudi Arabia, Iraq, Japan, South Korea, and India. In his first foreign visit, President Trump extracted from Saudi Arabia contracts for military equipment worth $100 billion. In his recent Asian trip to Japan and South Korea, Trump offered to sell "sophisticated military gear" so that these nations can defend themselves against North Korea, a country that has been carefully cultivated as a threat in the region. Consequently, Thaad missile defense launchers, missiles with payloads of up to 2,200 pounds, bunker-busting bombs, JAASM (long-range missiles), Spy-6 radar systems, and much more are for sale amounting to billions of dollars.

Congress first criticizes the arms deals that the president makes and then, after much sound and fury signifying nothing, approves them, leaving the impression among the simple-minded domestic and global audiences that the sale of military equipment is a favor that the U.S. does to its allies. Nothing is farther from the truth.

The warfare establishment is desperate to sell weapons, and worse, it has no moral qualms in fomenting international wars and civil insurrections in many parts of the planet. Wars sell weapons just as addictions sell drugs. A booming warfare industry creates jobs, wealth for shareholders, and supports the U.S. hegemonic policies. It also proves how the warfare establishment dupes the nations of the world.

The grand plan to sell warfare systems openly to allies and secretly to adversaries consists of a shrewd strategy. For years, the warfare establishment studies potential conflicts involving nations that can afford to buy weapons. For example, Saudi Arabia has been identified as a perfect candidate to engage in warfare with its neighbors. Saudi Arabia has a vulnerable monarchy. It is rich. In addition to domestic vulnerabilities, the war in Yemen, the Shia-Sunni discord, the disagreements with Qatar and Lebanon, and many other trigger points force Saudi Arabia to buy expensive weapons.

Creating the dread of Iran as the most dangerous, terror-sponsoring nation in the world fits into the establishment narrative that Saudi Arabia and the other Gulf States need to arm themselves against domestic revolutions and external aggression, all of it allegedly Iran-sponsored. Ironically, the dread of Iran also forces Israel to buy the U.S. warfare systems. The dread of Iran is beneficial for some European states willing to sell arms to Iran, after a "wink-wink" opposition from the U.S. warfare establishment. If Iran is militarily strong, the U.S. can sell more arms to its allies. This logic is so simple that the simple-minded finds it incredible.

Likewise, North Korea as a bully state in the region is conducive to selling arms to Japan and South Korea. The warfare establishment has every reason to showcase North Korea as a crazy country that can attack neighboring states without reason or warning. A cornered and demonized North Korea displays craziness of its own making (which country wouldn't under starvation pressures) but the warfare establishment blows it out of all proportion because the higher the dread, the higher the need for "defense" weapons that the U.S. warfare industry can sell for billions of dollars. To reinforce the dread of North Korea, the bogus conflict over the South China Sea is exaggerated to sell weapons to vulnerable states, including Taiwan.

As India emerges from poverty imposed by the British colonists and joins the top economies, the U.S. warfare establishment is drawing India into costly conflicts with China and Pakistan. The simmering territorial disputes with neighbors have been employed to persuade India to stand up to China and fight a cold war with Pakistan over Kashmir and Afghanistan. India has surged to the second biggest buyer of U.S. weapons.

President Trump, a guy seasoned in mischief, is a sharp merchant representing the warfare establishment for selling arms to nations of the world. Trump himself has no interest in minimizing international conflicts; and, moreover, the warfare establishment will not allow him to even think of a peaceful world where companies like Lockheed Martin, Northrop Grumman, Raytheon, General Dynamics, and L3 Technologies have no buyers.

An ungodly dog-eat-dog categorical imperative constructs an idyllic world for the U.S. warfare establishment to pursue hegemony, fake conciliations, and superpower duplicities. Some U.S. officials will play the role of peacemakers citing the Bible of love while the warfare establishment cooks and inflames deadly conflicts. "If you poison us, do we not die," complains Shylock in The Merchant of Venice.

22 Autumn in America

Few nations obtain the opportunity to lead the world of nearly two hundred nations of diverse cultures, histories, and economies. After the fall of the Soviet Union in 1991, the United States emerged as the sole superpower with formidable military and economic strengths. As a well-functioning democracy under which governments changed periodically and peacefully and where constitutional rights were being democratized for previously excluded communities, the United States was proving the thesis that liberty and prosperity can coexist within a decent legal system. Many highly gifted individuals all over the world viewed the United States as a miracle nation and wished to live and work here.

Gradually but steadily, arrogance misguided politicians and policy makers in Washington D.C. The presidency, congress, the military, and think-thanks — all dominated mostly by men intoxicated with power — embarked upon juvenile rhetoric and conduct that insulted diverse cultures, ridiculed world religions, and asserted raw power even in diplomatic circles of the United Nations. In 1995, Speaker of the House Newt Gingrich proclaimed with unmitigated hubris: "We're the only country complicated enough, sophisticated enough, big enough to lead the human race."

The 2001 terrorist attacks on the United States bamboozled the power-drivers in Washington D.C. The fall of the iconic twin towers and an assault on the Pentagon inflicted a national trauma anchored in disbelief, shaking the confidence in progressive American values. "The whole world is under the control of the evil" was the new consensus even among the highly educated secular elites, let alone the ordinary people indoctrinated with militaristic patriotism.

An erratic analysis of the "evil world" forced the United States into a self-squandering trajectory of war mongering. When an empire or a nation begins to fight the world through aggressive means, its tragic end is predictable. Recall how the Soviets invaded, occupied, and bullied Hungary (1956), Czechoslovakia (1968), and Afghanistan (1979), paving the way for its own demise. The U.S. invasions of Afghanistan (2001) and Iraq (2003), though vengeful and projections of power, were manifest errors.

Bombing villages in Afghanistan, destroying neighborhoods in Iraq, wholesale violations of human rights, and faith-based torture committed at Bagram, Abu Gharib, and Guantanamo shattered the morality of a superpower that lectured the whole world about the inherent dignity of human beings. Through inhumane invasions, America was losing its status as a beloved country of liberty and economic freedoms. The city on a hill, as President Ronald Reagan called the United States, turned off its lights.

Congress, more haughty and fitful than the presidency, has embarked on its own visionless path of imposing sanctions on various countries inviting ill-will and hatred of their people. Trade and financial sanctions rarely distinguish between friends and foes. Foes including Cuba, Iran, Russia, Venezuela, and Zimbabwe, and friends including Saudi Arabia, Pakistan, Egypt, and Mexico, all have been subject to various types of sanctions, embargos, and financial constraints. These sanctions have also been hurting the U.S. economy.

The rise of China as an enormous economic power is also quickening the self-squandering of the United States. While the United States armed forces are killing and getting killed in Afghanistan, China is investing in Afghanistan's natural resources. While the United States is drifting away from Pakistan, China is reconstructing the historic silk route with billions of dollars. While the United States is engrossed in military conflicts in Syria and Libya, China is weighing its options to rebuild these worn-torn countries. What the United States did to the Soviet Union, China is doing to the United States.

Having squandered its influence abroad, the United States is now turning on its own domestic future. The rise of Trumpism is more petrifying for the country's future than Trump's fatuous twittering. Trumpism as a phenomenon, though controversial, yearns to revive the "good old days" of a pre-1954 America (Brown v. Board of Education) (a case that outlawed apartheid) when non-white immigrants were fewer in number, when there were no mosques, when American-Japanese were interned, when blacks were under the white thumb, when women had little access to higher education and corporate America, and when there was no social pressure to recognize Spanish as a language.

Under Trumpism, diversity is turning into a dirty word. Ignoring contemporary ethnic complexity of the nation, employment hiring is blatantly reverting to dominant communities already disproportionately represented in corporations, universities, and government. Academic freedom is under attack as teachers and professors are harassed and punished for speaking up against hegemony of the National Rifle Association, for the rights of Palestinians, and for the dignity of Muslim women wearing religious hijab. The lands of Native Americans, whatever is left of them after centuries of theft, are being appropriated for laying fetid oil pipelines.

The promise of a complex and diverse America seems to have been torn apart. The Jeffersonian America of inalienable rights for all, once a cherished ideal, is being publicly mocked. Creatures like Carl Paladino and Bill O'Reilly are reinventing a bigoted America. Ugliness is replacing tolerance. Sentiments for secessions on part of various states, including Texas and California, though mere unpleasant rhetoric now, challenge the core integrity of the Union.

At this time of weakness both home and abroad, the slogan of Make America Great Again sounds much like the Siren Song in Homer's Odyssey. It is tragic entrapment for a shipwreck. Students of history know how nations squander to lose their God-gifted competitive military, economic, and moral advantage. The fall of the United States, and its possible dismemberment, will be yet another heart-rending story in human history.

ABOUT THE AUTHOR

Liaquat Ali Khan initially trained as a civil engineer. He later switched to law, obtaining a law degree from Punjab University, Lahore. In 1976, Khan immigrated to the United States and studied law at New York University School of Law where he received his LL.M. and J.S.D. Khan is admitted to the New York and Kansas Bars.

Khan has authored several books, including The Extinction of Nation-States (1996), A Theory of Universal Democracy (2003), A Theory of International Terrorism (2006), and Contemporary Ijtihad: Limits and Controversies (2011). Over the years, he has written numerous law review articles and essays on Islamic law, international law, commercial law, creative writing, legal humor, jurisprudence, the U.S. Constitution, comparative constitutional law, human rights, and foreign policy. His academic writings are used as part of course materials in universities across the world.

Khan has devoted much of his academic scholarship to Islamic law and conflicts involving Muslim communities. Khan has participated in Islamic law symposia held at various U.S. law schools—contributing ground-breaking articles on Islamic jurisprudence. In addition to law articles and academic books, Khan also writes for the popular press in the United States, the Middle East, and the Indian subcontinent. His legal and foreign affairs commentaries are published worldwide and international media, including BBC, Press TV, and NPR, seek his comments on world events.

Khan's writings are cited in various Wikipedia entries, including Sharia, Islamic democracy, nation-state, definitions of terrorism, and manual labor. In Spring 2007, Khan was a resident legal scholar with the Organization of Islamic Conference in Jeddah, Saudi Arabia. He has taught at Washburn University School of Law since 1983.

www.ingramcontent.com/pod-product-compliance
Lightning Source LLC
Chambersburg PA
CBHW031252250726
48655CB00005B/2195